Living
for
Eternity

Living for Eternity

EIGHT IMPERATIVES FROM SECOND PETER

Dave Breese

MOODY PRESS

CHICAGO

Library of Congress Cataloging in Publication Data

Breese, Dave, 1926-
    Living For Eternity.

    1. Christian life—1960-   . I. Title.
BV4501.2.B692   1988   248.4   87-35011
ISBN 0-8024-6632-X

2 3 4 5 6 7 8 Printing/BC/Year 93 92 91 90 89 88

Printed in the United States of America

To Carol,
the dearest on earth to me

Contents

Preface 9

Introduction 11

1. The High Road and the Low Road 17
2. The Imperative of Faith 29
3. The Imperative of Virtue 45
4. The Imperative of Knowledge 57
5. The Imperative of Self-Control 73
6. The Imperative of Patience 85
7. The Imperative of Godliness 99
8. The Imperative of Brotherly Kindness 111
9. The Imperative of Love 125
10. Moving On Up 137

Preface

No project like *Living for Eternity* is done alone. Ideas and convictions must be translated into the formulations of the mind. These must take the form of the spoken word. The spoken word must become the written word, and that, in my case, is done by the careful hands of others. My special, heartfelt thanks go to Terri Richter, enthusiastic typist and paragraph shaper, who has done the tedious work of manuscript typing, bringing these ideas to the printed page.

Sincere thanks to my wife, Carol, for her encouragement, her patient reading of the manuscript, and her spiritually perceptive suggestions throughout.

Genuine thanks are given to each member of our Christian Destiny staff, whose labors made possible our ongoing ministry during these days. In many cases, thoughts generated from their ideas found their way into these pages.

Some of the great learning experiences of my life have come from conversations with Christians across the nation and the world. They have blessed me with many of the concepts now presented in this book. Each member of the Christian community holds a genuine treasure— the insight into the Christian life that comes from the knowledge of Christ. Fortunate is the individual who has the opportunity to interact with many of these children of God. I have had that opportunity, and I consider myself fortunate indeed.

This book is presented with the hope and prayer that it will become a source of knowledge, spiritual motivation, and effective direction for those who read it. I invite responsible correspondence from readers concerning any of the matters presented here, for this book, as all valuable books, will doubtless produce a variety of reactions. It is written with the hope that it will cut through some of the ambiguities that distract the Body of Christ and beguile believers away from understanding the clear purpose of God for their lives. With these earnest hopes we present *Living for Eternity.*

Introduction

When a man says he will soon depart this life, his words catch our attention. We assume he will speak on matters he holds important. He will not give us a collection of tentative opinions or vague ideas. For him it is a serious time.

When the man making such an announcement is important, his last words gain added gravity. When presidents and kings address the nation, we listen. Their words impact culture and affect great numbers of people, both now and throughout generations to come. The farewell addresses of many statesmen are now revered as national treasures, the lore of a nation's history.

When the speaker is an apostle of Christ, he gains a new level of significance. His words are not to be discounted, for they contain truth of the highest gravity. They represent the crowning achievement of a faithful heart, the final statement of a mind infused with the mind of Christ. The words of a disciple who has spent much of his lifetime in the service of the King will be jewels of truth set in the gold crown of experience.

Then, when we recognize that the words are a part of holy Scripture, written under the inspiration of the Spirit of the living God, we know we are encountering truth that is more than important—it is imperative! When the writer himself says that we are to have "these things always in remembrance," what will we say? We must say nothing; we must listen. We must hear. We must heed. We must consider such words to be chiseled into the bedrock of Christian history—our history. We must find in them the answer to the most pressing question we as believers will face: "Lord, what will You have me to do?"

That is precisely the situation we encounter when we come to the words in 2 Peter 1:3-15, written by Peter shortly before his martyrdom in A.D. 67.

What a contrast between the foundational truth of Scripture and the elusive spirit of our age. Ours is a time that knows almost nothing of unchanging truth—truth that has application to our lives now and forever. As I once listened to a missionary friend speak soon after his return from five years' service in Latin America, he made a telling observation: "When I departed the country five years ago, I was used to the language and the expressions of that time. Now I have noticed that two words have grown in their usage so that they include nearly everything. These words are *casual* and *disposable*. Everything is now casual—our clothes, our conversations, and, yes, our convictions. All are casual. Everything is now disposable—the plates, the cups, the spoons. I suspect that that word now applies to our friends, our ethics, our promises—they too are disposable."

Casual and disposable. These two words could become the index of our time. We have casual clothing, casual shoes, casual friends, and (a common oxymoron) casual sex.

We have disposable flashlights and watches. But we also have disposable principles and disposable morals. We even have disposable parents and disposable children—especially the unborn.

Our times have become so unstable that even our preoccupied society has begun to take notice. In feeble response to the problem, some schools attempt to teach principles under a label such as "values clarification." But the hapless student is often told, "Do what is right for you," "Live by your personal principles," or, "Be honest with yourself." The poison of subjectivism is therefore injected more deeply into the mind of modern man, encouraging him to foolishly deny the possibility of objective values.

The existentialists have nearly carried the day. They are close to winning their war against meaning and rationality. All truth is now personal, all principles are negotiable, and all convictions are adaptable. The most solemn promises made among individuals or nations are now instantly subject to reconsideration "in the light of new developments." Truth—once believed to be eternal —is now reinterpreted "according to the changing context of life."

As the idea of the eternal slips from us, so too does the use of a word such as *imperative*. Because all things are temporal, passing quickly from the circle of our fascination, all things become trivial and incidental. Life no longer has duties, responsibilities, and obligations—only options. In the modern mind, the imperative has given way to the optional, the eternal to the incidental. The communicators of our time rent words for an evening; they borrow "truth" for a weekend and then quickly trade it in for a newer model. This generation leases its convictions until more modern, "truer" ones arrive from its adaptable pulpits or the fluid notions of academia.

Fluid notions—they are the modern substitute for foundational truth, the eternal truth of God. Thankfully, we as believers need not sacrifice our sanity on the pagan altars of this present scene. We have the open pages of Scripture. We need not force ourselves to live on the superficial ideas of "this present evil world" (Galatians 1:4). The Christian life is not trivial.

The apostle Peter, in his discourse on the imperatives of life, forcefully reminds us of the facts. He invites us to build a foundation that cannot be moved by the storms of time. He invites us to place upon that foundation the very pillars of Christian wisdom. He calls us to commitments that, he insists, bear within themselves the prospect of eternal reward. Let the world pursue its incidentals. It is our purpose to live our lives for eternity.

1

The High Road and the Low Road

While traveling here below, the believer does more than check off meaningless days. He progressively creates a record for eternity.

The child of God is a creature of eternal destiny. For him no day is without consequence, and no fleeting moment can be called incidental or unimportant. The hours he spends and the decisions he makes have implications that carry on into eternity. What he does today will matter a thousand years from today. The path of the just is like a shining light that shines more and more unto the perfect day (Proverbs 4:18).

With the ungodly it is not so. They are like the chaff that the wind drives away (Psalm 1:4). Even those who are most important on earth are, in the final analysis, no more than chaff from a threshing floor. The refuse may make an impressive pile, but with the next breeze it will disappear like a morning cloud.

The stories of those who refuse Christ and His salvation are accounts of wasted lives. They are made more tragic when we remember that for the unregenerate man life at its best is merely an unhappy prelude to a lost eternity. How sad that in this universe there should be so many who never aspire to live among the stars.

How sad also that even of those who aspire to "something more" here on earth, many never choose the golden staircase that begins at Calvary and leads to the Pleiades and beyond. Believing in their own abilities, leaning on the broken crutch of human possibilities, they miss the way of the cross. How different it could be! Futility is exchanged for eternal purpose when we place our faith in the finished work of Christ, completed on the cross for our redemption. To believe that Jesus Christ is the Son of God and that He died for our sins on Calvary's cross—that is what makes the eternal difference.

Salvation comes to us by grace alone, and all who believe in Christ are given the gift of eternal life, guaranteed by God. However, the path taken from salvation to heaven will not be the same for each child of God.

We are told in the Word of God that there is a difference, even for the Christian, in the roads that lead from here to the skies. So diverse are these paths that we could call them the high road and the low road. Of course, there are also many levels in between. Note the descriptions of two kinds of Christians in 2 Peter 1:8: "For if these things be in you, and abound, they make you that ye shall neither be barren nor unfruitful in the knowledge of our Lord Jesus Christ." That is the high road. "But he that lacketh these things is blind, and cannot see afar off, and hath forgotten that he was purged from his old sins" (v. 9). That is the low road.

How important is the earnest call? "Wherefore the rather, brethren, give diligence to make your calling and election sure: for if ye do these things, ye shall never fall: for so an entrance shall be ministered unto you abundantly into the everlasting kingdom of our Lord and Saviour Jesus Christ" (vv. 10-11).

What a startling, frightening, important contrast! The believer who travels the high road to heaven, who builds "these things" Peter speaks of into his life, will be welcomed into the glory of heaven in a spectacular fashion. The citizens of the Roman Empire understood what that meant. Those who lived in Rome had seen the spectacular occasions on which a victorious commander of the Roman legions was welcomed home. The emperor declared a national holiday, and all of the citizens of Rome, bedecked in their best apparel, gathered at the gate to meet him. When the preparations were completed, the general marched his legions through the gate into the city amid the applause of admiring crowds. The bands played, the dancers performed, and the city rejoiced at the returning legion and its commander, who brought with them the laurels of victory.

The general kissed the hand of the emperor and officially delivered to him his addition to the empire, conquered and subdued through his skill and courage. The citizens rejoiced in that the emperor was glorified and the kingdom strengthened by the worthy commander they celebrated.

It was customary for the emperor to lavish gifts upon the commander and soldiers. Large sums of money, usually the spoils of victory, would be distributed to the legionnaires. The commander, proportionate to the extent of his conquests, was given cities to rule, political office, fame, and glory. Upon special occasions, he was made a ruler second only to the emperor himself. Rome knew how to reward its best servants, which is partly why it was for hundreds of years the greatest kingdom on earth.

Such celebrations, well-known in Bible times, offer an appropriate illustration of the believer's arrival in heaven. Rewards are promised again and again in the Word of God to those who serve Him well. Best of all, the faithful child of God can anticipate the greatest reward of all: the privilege of hearing the emperor of the universe say, "Well done, thou good and faithful servant: . . . enter thou into the joy of thy lord" (Matthew 25:21).

But Peter presents an alternate picture as well. The unfaithful, insensitive believer can expect no such glorious entrance into heaven. The stodgy, slovenly traveler on the road of life must be content with lesser rewards or, worse, none at all. Lacking "these things," he is blind. Even during his journey in this world, he will stumble along on the rocks, a bruised and bleeding traveler. Because of his blindness—or at least his nearsightedness—he can be expected to take wrong turns, losing his way in the brambles and the ditches. If he continues in his spiritual myopia, he will be ever confused, frustrated, and depressed over the lack of progress in his painful journey.

When he finally arrives in heaven, he will be saved yet as by fire. No abundant entrance, no great congratulation will be his. Yes, he will have salvation, his solely by the grace of God. But the rewards of sacrifice and selfless service will escape him. He may bring, in his presumptions, a few pieces of wood, hay, and stubble, but they will quickly disappear, unable to stand the test of the fire.

In this passage from the last letter of the apostle Peter there is an earnest message for each of us today. We commonly hear reports that Christianity has a billion followers. Of this number, how many have given evidence that they are truly converted? How many have been saved by faith in the crucified One? Certainly not all.

But what of those who are truly converted, having exercised saving faith in the Lord Jesus Christ? How many are traveling with clear vision along the high road? On the ridges the air is pure, and the sunlight of purpose shines bright. How many live above the fog, able to see far off where the walls of the celestial city shine and the King eternal lives? Certainly not all.

In fact, who could have predicted such a day as this within the Body of Christ? Who could have foreseen the disturbed lives, the broken homes, the distressed youth, and the depressed adults who populate the church? Who could have foreseen the many who succeed materially but fail spiritually? We have reached the point at which our great churches and attractive homes can no longer hide the heartbreak that ravages them from within.

Furthermore, who could have foreseen the duplicity and foolishness that have been embraced and practiced by Christians, even at a leadership level? How many have begun as humble ministers of Christ and then heaped the shrine of luxury, pride and lasciviousness with incense kindled at the Spirit's flame? Pity the blind; but do not appoint them to be the guides for the journey.

Their condition need not, however, be permanent. Christian history is filled with accounts of those who testify that, even after they came to know Christ, they were spiritually blind. Then came the moment when they began to diligently pursue the will of God, and a clear vision of His purpose overtook them. They experienced "the high calling of God in Christ Jesus" (Philippians 3:14), and their lives took on a level they had never known before.

The call to the high road is extended to all. The high calling of God in Christ Jesus must be heard anew by the church and by each Christian. We must concentrate more intently on what Peter calls "these things." Such concentration will, we are promised, produce spiritual success in time and divine congratulation in eternity.

What are "these things"? What are the things with which our Christian life is an eternal success and without which we are blind and stumbling? We can rejoice in the fact that they are not mysterious, nameless feelings, forces, or fantasies promised only to a select few. Peter presents them faithfully and clearly in his letter to us. They are: faith, virtue, knowledge, self-control, patience, godliness, brotherly kindness, and love. In the pursuit of these, we are enjoined, yes, *commanded* to be diligent.

Diligence calls us to study seriously and consider carefully the words of Scripture. It forbids us to waste time pursuing lesser things, especially the meaningless, repetitive spiritual projects so common to our time.

Diligence forbids the idleness that is common to many Christians today. How easily we allow the days to become months and the months years with nothing of consequence accomplished for the Savior. Yes, we have dreams. We have intentions. We have hopes, anticipations, and ambitions. None of these, however, produces anything but frustration unless we are *doing* what we dream, *producing* what we intend. Without this production, the dreams of a slothful man tend to destroy him, because his hands refuse to labor. Dreams must not become the master of our lives.

Before us are the imperatives, the path to them is diligence. We must note, however, that these qualities are not "the inevitables." The Christian will not *inevitably* grow in grace, live a spiritually successful life, and arrive in heaven to congratulations. If the imperatives were inevitable, there would be no need for the call to diligence.

This truth must not be missed. One may hear leaders, preachers, and well-meaning believers say, "If he doesn't go straight and achieve virtue, knowledge, and these other marks of a believer, he is simply not a Christian." How often have we heard the expression, "If Christ is not Lord of all, He is not Lord at all"?

Such a perspective is spiritually misleading. Salvation comes to us in the form of a ransom; we are purchased from our sins. The call to spiritual achievement is extended to *the Christian.*

One who insists that we are saved by the lives we live is saying that the great qualities we are called to add to our lives are, in fact, inevitable in the life of all Christians. This view leads us to one of the many systems of salvation by works invading the church today. "You must do this or that, or you are not a Christian!" is the frightening cry of those who succumb to this position.

The *inevitable* consequence of saving faith is eternal life, that great gift from God. Salvation is the gift of God to me, purchased with the sufficient blood of Christ. Spiritual success is my gift to Him, purchased with diligence, the singular pursuit of His plan, when I might have done otherwise. It comes, as D. L. Moody said, from "my human best, filled with the spirit of God."

In our pursuit of the imperatives we have as our shining example Jesus Christ Himself. In the course of His ministry, Christ did not travel casually and aimlessly from one place to another. He did not seek out the superficial subjects that characterize so many of our conversations. His entire life was the diligent pursuit of one goal.

The life of Christ was not a set of happy accidents. It was the plan of God combined with the intense and singular effort of the Son, designed to accomplish those things without which the world would die. Jesus Christ is more than merely the greatest man who ever lived. He is the one person the world could not have done without.

Christ diligently pursued the imperatives. Matthew reported, "From that time forth began Jesus to shew unto his disciples, how that he must go unto Jerusalem, and suffer many things of the elders and chief priests and scribes, and be killed, and be raised again the third day" (Matthew 16:21). Note the use of the word *must*. There was simply no alternative!

Our Lord could have taken a holiday at the seashore in Galilee or a vacation on the Mediterranean for needed rest and contemplation. He had many options, but none of them took priority over His mission. He said He *must* go to Jerusalem, for the purpose of His life was to give Himself a ransom for many. Apart from His fulfillment of that purpose, there would be no redemption.

This purpose was clear to Him, but not to His disciples, as we see from Peter's response to Christ's statement: "Then Peter took him, and began to rebuke him, saying, Be it far from thee, Lord: this shall not be unto thee. But he turned, and said unto Peter, Get thee behind me, Satan: thou art an offence unto me: for thou savourest not the things that be of God, but those that be of men" (vv. 22-23).

We see how anxious Satan was to divert Him from God's plan. He used Peter's voice and sympathies in an attempt to dissuade Christ from accomplishing His purpose. Christ recognizes this in His denunciation of Peter: "Get thee behind me, Satan: thou art an offence unto me" (v. 23). Peter did not understand the imperative nature of Christ's mission, for he did not understand the things of God.

Satan will try to use the same program of spiritual subversion on you and me. It is his goal to take us from imperative living to inconsequential living. How many a potentially great servant of God has been beguiled away from God's path because he heeded the voice of the devil, sometimes coming through the lips of a friend, saying, "Be it far from thee." Had our Lord not committed Himself to accomplish the imperative of His life, there would be no salvation. Had He turned aside to other pursuits, the story of the world would be a far different and infinitely more dismal one. To turn aside from the pursuit of the imperatives is to turn from the accomplishment of God's purpose for us. It is to guarantee spiritual failure.

Christ demonstrated the same degree of purposefulness when He spoke of taking the gospel to the world. He said, "Other sheep I have, which are not of this fold: them also I must bring, and they shall hear my voice; and there shall be one fold, and one shepherd" (John 10:16). Again He used the word *must*. This task is not optional for Him—or for us. If we need a motivation for taking the gospel to a lost world, we need look no further than the words "them also I must bring."

Must we not do the same? The Christian community dedicates itself to a thousand optional activities. These may be fulfilling, fascinating, and even good by some standards. However, we must not ignore the warning that "the good is the enemy of the best." Doing "good things" may make our lives more interesting and bring us the congratulations of others. But doing those things consumes time, energy, and money and may prevent us from accomplishing the *great* work God has appointed us to do. To give ourselves to lesser things is to prevent those greater things from being realized.

Once when visiting the home of my pastor and mentor, Lance B. Latham, I saw a striking illustration of this. Before we sat down to a lovely dinner, Lance took perhaps twenty minutes to play the piano. His talent and ability were apparent as he played pieces by Bach, Beethoven, and other great masters. He followed that with beautiful renditions of some great hymns.

I was still lost in the mood of it when Lance turned to me with a look of pensiveness on his face. He made the astonishing remark, "Dave, only God saved me from music." He was saying that music—while something magnificent—was for him less important than preaching the gospel. There are few Bible teachers today who can teach the book of Romans the way he could. There are none who believe it with a greater passion than he did. The world might live without music, but it could not survive apart from justification by faith.

Lance B. Latham pursued many of the higher things of life. His ultimate diligence and dedication, however, was reserved for the accomplishment of his ultimate mission. That was to preach and teach the Word of God in the most effective way possible to as many as possible. The results of that dedication continue in the lives of multitudes across the world today.

Our Lord spoke clearly to would-be followers who insisted that they must bury their fathers, get married, buy a piece of land, or perform another otherwise legitimate pursuit before they could follow Him. He told them they could not do both (Luke 9:57-62). An athlete may profess adequate ability in a number of sports. However, he will never become a world-class athlete in any one sport until he focuses his attention there and says, "This one thing I will do!" Likewise, we cannot expect to become world-class Christians until we know the meaning of the word *diligence* and put it into practice as we seek to live for eternity.

Faith

2

The Imperative of Faith

There are many precious things in this world. Some, such as diamonds, pearls, homes, cars, coins, and other valuables can be looked upon or held in the hand. Others, intangible and more difficult to perceive, become more valuable than the tangible things upon reflection. These include citizenship, safety, health, friendships, and relationships of various kinds. Without the intangibles, the tangibles would quickly lose their value. The wise person looks to the things that are unseen as well as the things that are seen. The things seen are temporal, but the things not seen are eternal.

God has told us that the first imperative, the most basic quality in the world, is faith. When beginning his discourse on the eight imperatives of life Peter names the first imperative: faith. We will begin by adding to our faith.

What is faith? How does it work in life? Why is it so important? These questions have been asked by Christians in every century. Because we are prone to believe what we see, confidence in something unseen seems mysterious. God repeatedly admonishes us to be not faithless but believing. We are called to accept divine truth and reject human falsehood. Often, however, the visible and appealing falsehood wins the race to capture our attention with the help of the evil one, who is a liar from the beginning. Thus the visible triumphs over the invisible, and we are deceived.

To discover the meaning of faith (the ability to perceive and the courage to believe the invisible things of God) and to anchor our souls in its solid substance is the beginning of understanding and the key to salvation itself.

To understand the imperative of faith we must remember that faith can be understood in at least two ways. The first way to understand it is as "the faith."

This aspect of faith is implied by Peter's opening statement in 2 Peter. He said he was writing "to them that have obtained like precious faith with us through the righteousness of God and our Saviour Jesus Christ" (1:1). Faith, in this sense, was referred to by Christ when He asked the question, "When the Son of man cometh, shall he find [the] faith on the earth?" (Luke 18:8). Clear also is the call that we are to be "established in the faith" (Acts 16:5). Indeed, the importance of this faith is emphasized by the reminder that in the last days, some shall depart from "the faith" (1 Timothy 4:1).

Faith is therefore presented in the Bible as, first of all, the body of truth that Christians believe. "The faith" is that set of facts, revealed in Scripture, dealing with the reality of God and man's relationship to Him. They must be understood, because there can be no personal faith without "the faith."

What then is the body of truth that constitutes the faith? The foundations of the Christian faith include the following:

1. *There is a God.* The Bible teaches that above and beyond all other considerations in life stands one prime fact: God is. The first revelation of Scripture is "In the beginning God" (Genesis 1:1).

Having revealed Himself in nature and in the Bible, God has told us that He is omnipotent, omniscient, omnipresent, and is before all things. To become established in the faith, the inquirer would do well to open the pages of Scripture and read of how God has announced His existence and told us about Himself.

Under the first principle, then, we establish ourselves as theists and not atheists. We believe that God is.

2. *God is a Trinity.* The Lord has revealed Himself as eternally existent in three persons: Father, Son, and Holy Spirit. God has not explained to us how the Trinity is possible, for the word *possible* is only relevant to man. With God, nothing is impossible. Nevertheless, we have His word for it—God is three Persons and yet One. We Christians are not unitarians; we are trinitarians.

3. *God created the universe.* We know that the universe is not a self-existent entity that has always been and will always be. Rather, it was created out of nothing by the Lord Himself. To speak precisely, the world was created by Jesus Christ Himself. When Scripture refers to Christ it says, "For by him were all things created, that are in heaven, and that are in earth, visible and invisible, whether they be thrones, or dominions, or principalities, or powers: all things were created by him, and for him: and he is before all things, and by him all things consist" (Colossians 1:16-17).

We Christians, therefore, believe that creation is to be respected but not worshiped. We are not pantheists (who are, in essence, no different from atheists).

4. *Sin has come into the world.* Man was made in the image of God. That image, however, was defaced when Eve and then Adam ate the fruit forbidden to them by God. Scripture says, "By one man sin entered into the world, and death by sin; and so death passed upon all men, for that all have sinned" (Romans 5:12).

As Christians, therefore, we must recognize that the sublime creation of God has been defaced by the cancer called sin. Sin has separated man from God, making it utterly impossible for human beings to have fellowship with the Lord except through the loving provision God has provided in the sacrifice of Christ on the cross.

5. *Jesus Christ is the Son of God.* With this affirmation, we come close to the core of Christianity. It is the conviction that Jesus Christ, born of a virgin, was indeed Emmanuel, God with us. We are sure that God was in Christ and that He came for the purpose of reconciling the world to Himself.

The deity of Christ is one of the most fundamental buildings blocks of the faith. Marvelous vitality comes into the life of a person whose deepest conviction is the deity of Christ. "Who is he that overcometh the world, but he that believeth that Jesus is the Son of God?" (1 John 5:5). As the Son of God, Jesus Christ is the Lord of history, and the provision He made for our salvation is sure and steadfast.

6. *Christ offers salvation through His blood.* We Christians are sure that the center point of history is a place called Calvary and that history's greatest event transpired there. At Calvary Jesus Christ took on Himself the sins of the world. Indeed, He was made sin for us with the marvelous result that we should receive the gift of imputed righteousness. It is Calvary that becomes the

sole basis of our salvation. The Christian means it when he sings, "Calvary covers it all" and "pardon there was multiplied to me." It is the blood of Jesus Christ, God's Son, that cleanses from all sin.

7. *Salvation comes to the sinner by faith alone.* The essence of Christianity is that salvation is by faith. In a sense, there are only two religions in the world—Christianity and all others. In one way or another, the religions of the world (and even some that are called Christianity) teach the production of human righteousness, the winning of merit before God on the basis of human works.

True Christianity, however, presents the gift of "righteousness without works" (Romans 4:6) to all who will exercise faith in the finished work of Christ on Calvary's cross.

As Christians, we identify with the words of Robert Murray McCheyne in "Jehovah Tsidkenu":

> I once was a stranger to grace and to God,
> I knew not my danger and felt not my load;
> Though friends spoke in rapture of Christ on the
>   tree,
> Jehovah Tsidkenu* was nothing to me.
>
> I oft read with pleasure, to soothe or engage,
> Isaiah's wild measure and John's simple page.
> But e'en when they pictured the blood-sprin-
>   kled tree,
> Jehovah Tsidkenu seemed nothing to me.
>
> Like tears from the daughters of Zion that roll,
> I wept when the waters went over His soul;
> Yet thought not that my sins had nailed to the tree
> Jehovah Tsidkenu—'twas nothing to me.

*"The Lord our righteousness."

When free grace awoke me, by light from on
   high,
Then legal fear shook me, I trembled to die;
No refuge, no safety in self could I see—
Jehovah Tsidkenu my Saviour must be.

My terrors all vanished before the sweet name;
My guilty fears banished, with boldness I came
To drink at the fountain, life-giving and free—
Jehovah Tsidkenu is all things to me.

Jehovah Tsidkenu! my treasure and boast,
Jehovah Tsidkenu! I ne'er can be lost;
In Thee I shall conquer by flood and by field—
My cable, my anchor, my breastplate and shield!

Even treading the valley, the shadow of death,
This watchword shall rally my faltering breath;
For while from life's fever my God sets me free,
Jehovah Tsidkenu, my death-song shall be.

Beyond these basics, the Bible teaches many things
about the faith. We can see that, above all other things,
Christianity is a doctrinal religion. By that we mean it is a
presentation of facts about actual people and events in
history. Above every other consideration, it is a body of
truth most surely to be believed.

No one is a Christian apart from believing this body
of truth. An individual may be winsome, good, fine, and
decent, but he is not a Christian because of those qualities. Nothing about ourselves makes us Christians. We
are Christians only by the fact that we hold true objective
facts about Jesus Christ and His finished work on the
cross. There can be no faith, then, without "the faith."

We might illustrate these facts by noting that we
live in intransitive times. From our high school English

classes, we remember that an intransitive verb is one that does not take an object. A transitive verb, therefore, is one that does take an object. There is a definite erosion in the English language today. In one such deviation, we have begun to use transitive verbs as if they were intransitive.

In the realm of religion, this tendency is practiced every day. We are told to have faith, but we are not told in whom or in what to have faith. We are told to pray without being told what or who should be the object of our prayers. We are counseled to "just believe" without being given an object of that belief. We are advised to trust without being told that it is impossible to trust without trusting something or someone. Under the influence of these existential times, Christianity itself is believed by some to be a faith that takes no object and is anchored in nothing. It then becomes the emotion of a moment, the good feeling of an evening, or a fleeting sense of the presence of God. Consequently, the salvation claimed by some could be without foundation. It may be nothing more than an imagined psychological experience with an imaginary Jesus.

Let us remember, then, that faith without "the faith" is delusion. Above all else, Christianity, the call to faith, presents the divine Person and the historical acts in which to believe.

As a result of this historical, objective faith, it is possible for us to have personal faith. That is what Peter is referring to when he says to "add to your faith" the other imperatives. He assumes that his readers have moved from cynicism to acceptance and have stepped from no faith to the faith.

Christianity is, therefore, not only "the faith," but it is personal, subjective faith. When I exercise faith, the objective facts about God and the atonement available in Jesus Christ become my personal possessions.

Each person must ask himself, *Do I have this personal faith? What is personal, saving faith in Christ?*

This "faith unto salvation" has been illustrated in many ways. If I stand on the twenty-seventh floor of a tall building and press the button for an elevator, I am confident (I have faith) that the elevator will arrive. Indeed, it does, and the door opens. I am now presented with a vehicle that, I am confident (I have faith), will take me to the ground floor or to the top of that building, provided I step into it. When I do, my faith in that elevator takes the form of *personal* trust. It has become not only objective confidence but a personal reality to me.

In the same way, the faith of the gospel—the truth of Christianity—becomes the path to my personal salvation when I exercise faith. This is accomplished by accepting Christ's death as my way to right standing before God.

This way of salvation is presented to us by the apostle John when he gives us his account of the life and ministry of Christ. He speaks of the Lord Jesus coming into the world to His own people and making them the loving offer of salvation. Sadly, their response was negative: "He came unto his own, and his own received him not" (John 1:11). This is one of the saddest verses in the Bible.

Because they did not receive Him, Israel—and then the world—moved into desolation and rejection.

But then comes one of the happiest verses in Scripture. There were individuals who did hear and heed and who believed the facts about the Lord Jesus. "But as many as received him, to them gave he power to become the sons of God, even to them that believe on his name" (John 1:12). Exercising faith comes in the form of receiving Christ—believing on His name.

Christ illustrated this transaction further when, explaining the way of salvation, He said, "As Moses lifted up the serpent in the wilderness, even so must the Son of man be lifted up: that whosoever believeth in him should not perish, but have eternal life" (John 3:14-15). In referring back to this Old Testament picture, Christ is using an event in the lives of the children of Israel to show the nature of personal acceptance of Him.

In Numbers 21 we see that the children of Israel committed a transgression against the Lord. In that regard, they are an illustration of the entire human race and of each one of us. They spoke against the Lord, and they held His provision for them in contempt. They said, "For there is no bread, neither is there any water; and our soul loatheth this light bread" (Numbers 21:5). The response from the Lord is most telling. "The Lord sent fiery serpents among the people, and they bit the people; and much people of Israel died" (v. 6).

As a result of this judgment, there was the responsive conviction of sin on the part of the people. We have here an illustration of the purpose of God's judgment of the world. "Therefore the people came to Moses, and said, We have sinned, for we have spoken against the Lord, and against thee; pray unto the Lord, that he take away the serpents from us. And Moses prayed for the people" (v. 7).

What was the provision that came from God? "The Lord said unto Moses, Make thee a fiery serpent, and set it upon a pole: and it shall come to pass, that every one that is bitten, when he looketh upon it, shall live" (v. 8).

What an interesting and marvelous provision! The Lord instructed Moses that a serpent resembling the one that bit the people was to be made of brass. To obtain healing, the people were required only to look upon the serpent. The formula that came from God was "Look and live."

Moses did as he was instructed, putting a serpent on a pole in the center of the camp and inviting those who were infected to participate in the divine remedy. What a beautiful result came to pass! "If a serpent had bitten any man, when he beheld the serpent of brass, he lived" (v. 9). The message that went out to the people of Israel was that God had provided a way by which they would be delivered. The requirement placed upon them was so simple as to be almost unrelated to the severity of the problem.

Now there may have been those in Israel who had philosophic arguments against this method of deliverance, who believed that other remedies were superior, or who allowed personal disillusionment or a dozen other problems to prevent them from believing and responding to this simple remedy. However, no other provision had been made except that one must look and then one would live. The simple way of salvation was also the sole way of salvation.

Christ used this account of the serpent in the wilderness to illustrate saving faith. He announced that in this very fashion must "the Son of man be lifted up: that whosoever believeth in him should not perish, but have eternal life" (John 3:14-15).

Following this statement comes that magnificent offer of eternal life. Jesus gives us the most well-known and revered statement in the entire Word of God, "For God so loved the world, that he gave his only begotten Son, that whosoever believeth in him should not perish, but have everlasting life" (v. 16). Christ then tells us that the Son of Man came not to bring condemnation but salvation. Salvation becomes mine through faith.

The simplicity of faith is also evident in the life of Abraham. In Romans 4:1-2 the apostle Paul says, "What shall we say then that Abraham our father, as pertaining to the flesh, hath found? For if Abraham were justified by works, he hath whereof to glory; but not before God. For what saith the scripture? Abraham believed God, and it was counted unto him for righteousness."

Abraham is the illustration of the exercise of saving faith. What did Abraham actually do in order to receive imputed righteousness? He believed God. The word used here is *amen*. Abraham said amen to God, and he was instantly and eternally saved, having received the gift of imputed righteousness.

Paul presses the point by saying, "Now to him that worketh is the reward not reckoned of grace, but of debt. But to him that worketh not, but believeth on him that justifieth the ungodly, his faith is counted [imputed] for righteousness" (vv. 4-5). Salvation, then, comes not to the one who works to earn or merit the gift. It is given to the one who believes. Faith alone brings imputed righteousness.

What is imputed righteousness? It is merit or acceptance before God that is put to our account, as it were, in the bank of heaven. It is not imparted righteousness, for there is no such thing. In salvation, God does not *make* us righteous, but He *declares* us righteous. Imputed righteousness, therefore, is the basis of our perfect *legal* standing before God. Because of this ascribed righteousness "there is therefore now no condemnation to them which are in Christ Jesus" (Romans 8:1).

Down through the years of Christian history, thousands convicted of sin, conscious that they have offended God, wanting to be reconciled to Him, have asked the question, What must I do to be saved? Many discovered, even in the process of asking this question, the trust that became personal faith in the Savior.

From where does this faith come? "Faith cometh by hearing, and hearing by the word of God" (Romans 10:17). We can promise that the one who examines the teaching of the Scripture with an open mind will become aware of the need for faith. In the sincere seeker, this awareness will produce the desire for personal salvation. That desire, followed by the exercise of personal faith, brings the seeker to the transaction that is salvation.

From faith where do we go?

Having been saved by faith, the believer discovers faith to be a growing thing. God increasingly becomes the loving Father who rules our lives and who is to be trusted in every circumstance and with everything. Having come to Christ, the apostle Paul tells of the consequences of his own personal step of faith. He said, "I know whom I have believed, and am persuaded that he is able to keep that which I have committed unto him against that day" (2 Timothy 1:12). By faith we can trust God not only for eternal salvation but for every other consideration in life as well.

In exactly this fashion, Paul, in the name of the Lord, extends an invitation to us. In his most brilliant treatise, the book of Romans, he speaks to those who have believed and says, "I beseech you therefore, brethren, by the mercies of God, that ye present your bodies a living sacrifice, holy, acceptable unto God, which is your reasonable service" (Romans 12:1). Here the call to commitment is not extended to the sinner but to the brethren. Salvation and commitment are two distinct things. Eternal life comes because of Christ's commitment unto death for us on the cross. Significant service for the Savior comes when our faith leads us to commitment to Him.

Faith, therefore, is the door to salvation and the basis of all the qualities that God intends to build faithfully into our lives. So imperative is this first quality of life that it is presented in the Word of God as the basis of life itself. Consequently, we have the oft-repeated principle in Scripture "the just shall live by faith" (Romans 1:17). By faith we anticipate that we will live through each day. By faith we retire at night in the quiet confidence that we shall wake in the morning. By faith we cross the street, drive a car, ride on an airplane, and perform a hundred other daily tasks. The one who insists that he wants nothing to do with faith and claims that he operates only on the basis of his eyes will find it impossible to live at all. Those who deny the existence of faith and claim they rely only on what can be seen and proved are deluding themselves. It takes faith for anyone to live. The Christian, however, knows that and rejoices in it.

When the Christian decides to live by faith, to rest in its inevitability, he makes a wonderful discovery. He discovers that he has access by faith into the grace wherein he stands (Romans 5:2). Before him opens the treasure house of God, access to everything, including the universe itself, which has been purchased for him by Jesus Christ on Calvary's cross. The promise given to us by the apostle Paul has yet to be tested to its fullest by even the most ambitious Christian. "Therefore being justified by faith, we have peace with God through our Lord Jesus Christ: by whom also we have access by faith into this grace wherein we stand, and rejoice in hope of the glory of God" (Romans 5:1-2). Walking by faith should not be a tenuous and trembling activity on the part of the timid, reluctant believer. It should produce great accomplishments and rejoicing in what Scripture calls the "hope of the glory of God." The believer who moves from a tentative pursuit of the will of God to enthusiastic participation in the life of faith can expect astonishing results.

In Hebrews 11 God has given us the believers' hall of fame. Here we can read the stories of Abel, Enoch, Noah, Abraham, Joseph, Moses, and many others. The heroic lives of these spiritual giants reinforce what we already know but need to remember: "Without faith it is impossible to please him: for he that cometh to God must believe that he is, and that he is the rewarder of them that diligently seek him" (Hebrews 11:6). Just a glimpse into the possibilities of faith should lead us to say with sincerity to our heavenly Father, "Lord, increase our faith."

Virtue

3

The Imperative of Virtue

"**A**dd to your faith virtue" (2 Peter 1:5). In Peter's list of imperatives, the first to be added to faith is perhaps the rarest. It is virtue.

In some ways virtue could also be called the most necessary. Virtue is the quality that places its stamp upon all other qualities in life. To fail at virtue is to fail at everything. A man may be talented, knowledgeable, capable, and characterized by remarkable ability in many ways. However, if he is not believed to be virtuous, he will hardly be trusted, even in the performance of his highest abilities. He will fail.

We know from our deepest instincts (the work of God within us) that the basis of life is moral. The world, in the last analysis, is not made of bricks and stones or even atoms and molecules. It is made of a substance that, in its essence, is moral.

This must be so, because the Maker of the universe is God Himself. This God, whom we know and worship, has declared Himself to be, first of all, a *holy* God. The people and things that will ultimately prosper in such a universe are those that are morally compatible with the nature of God. The people and things that will ultimately fail and be destroyed are those that set themselves at variance to the nature of God. It may be said of those attempting to beat the system that, when the system is designed by God Himself, it simply cannot be done.

The call to virtue, then, is the earnest and immediate invitation to those who have put their faith in Christ. What is virtue? How can we add it to our lives? Why is it imperative?

Virtue is not a simple thing. The word in Scripture means "intrinsic eminence, moral goodness." But virtue is not simply morality. Morality is the successful measuring up to a standard given to us and is a component of virtue. But virtue is more than that. It means "doing good things" as well as "not doing bad things." Virtue refers to the *being* of a person; it is his ever-increasing moral ability.

It is more than just doing a good thing now and then. It is more than doing good things fairly regularly. It is the achieved state whereby the soul operates on a level of goodness itself. It is characterized by abstinence, yes; good works, yes. Virtue is a moral reliability that becomes synonymous with our life-style. The virtuous person would not be *believed* to have done an evil thing, despite reports to the contrary.

"Sally Jones would *never* do a thing like that" is a profound statement. It is a most awesome compliment. The speaker may not know by external or legal evidence whether Sally did or did not do the thing. He simply "knows" that she would *never* entertain such a thought.

Virtue, therefore, comes close to what the world calls character. It is the regular practice of goodness that brings a certain condition to the soul. It is not an isolated breakthrough into goodness but a perennial state.

Let us consider the difference between an isolated breakthrough and a perennial state. Suppose you were to attend a big-league ballpark and find, to your astonishment, that I was playing on one of the teams. Let us say that I came to bat and promptly hit the ball into the left field stands. You might say, "My, that Dave Breese can certainly play baseball!" But you would be wrong.

You would be wrong in that what you had seen was an isolated breakthrough, not a perennial state. If you knew my batting average, you would correctly assume that I was an interloper, wearing someone else's uniform on the baseball field. You might assume that you had observed a publicity stunt rather than the real thing. And you would be correct.

By contrast, let us say that I went to the ballpark back long ago and saw Babe Ruth play without knowing who he was. Let us say that I saw the Babe strike out. I might assume that he was a poor athlete and wonder why he was on the team. "He's no good," I might say. But I would be wrong. What I saw would have been a temporary defection from a high level of baseball ability.

That's the way it is with virtue. Virtue is a high state of moral ability perfected over the years by walking with God. Virtue is a condition whereby any day, any night, any weekend, we can be sure that the virtuous person is living a righteous life, no matter what pressures may be placed upon him.

How necessary are such lives today. How important it is for millions of Christians to add virtue to their faith. We may mouth great and resounding words about Christianity and the Bible. We may claim gifts and point to vast experience. All of our claims are like sounding brass or a tinkling cymbal if we have not added virtue to our faith.

The call to virtue is particularly vital when we think of it in the midst of our present society. In other eras of Christian history, the believer could rely on support systems to help him toward the life of virtue. Families stayed intact. The church took a community form. The neighborhood itself enjoyed a higher measure of common grace and ethical living. Believers stayed in closer contact with others of the faith.

Our society, with its drastic degeneration, has moved to the place where it has no use for virtue. The support systems that were an aid to virtue have disintegrated, giving way to a society that is essentially subversive to moral goodness. The world has devised a thousand means to produce moral destruction in the lives of its individuals. This generation is being pressed upon with more opportunities to sin at a younger age and in increasingly clever ways.

How, then, can we build into our lives that moral strength called virtue? The first course of action is clear—we must call on the Father for help.

Before coming to Christ, each of us was a confirmed sinner. The Bible says that there is not a just man upon the earth or one who does not sin (Romans 3:23). Men love darkness rather than light because their deeds are evil, and they continue to do evil. The apostle Paul refers to himself as well as others when he refers to the days before he came to the Savior: "We all had our conversation in times past in the lusts of our flesh, fulfilling the desires of the flesh and of the mind; and were by nature the children of wrath, even as others" (Ephesians 2:3). To this day, every person who does not know the Lord is subject to the continued, daily debilitations of sin. Finally, he cannot help himself and becomes an addict to iniquity.

This has happened in our time, not only to individuals, but to our culture as well. In this generation we have seen a frighteningly vast number turn to iniquity. Indeed, we have seen come to pass in our society the fulfillment of Alexander Pope's dictum:

> Vice is a monster of such hideous mein
> As to be hated needs but to be seen
> But seen too oft, familiar with her face
> We first endure, then pity, then embrace.

Vice has become endemic in our time. Indeed, by every standard for measuring iniquity our generation wins first prize. Whether it be robbery, murder, rape, pillage, arson, revolution, violence, drug addiction, white-collar corruption—our generation wins in the stakes of high iniquity.

This generation, for want of virtue, is not only sinful but also shameless. To sin is one thing, but to sin shamelessly is another. The person who knows that sin is sin may be led to repentance. For the sinner who calls sin "righteousness" and adultery "sexual preference" there is little hope. Sinfulness is a great evil, but shamelessness is evil personified. It is, in fact, reprobation.

This generation is well described in 2 Peter 2:13 as "they that count it pleasure to riot [revel] in the day time." The things people were once ashamed to do in the darkness of midnight, they now do proudly at noon. The things over which society once cringed in shame are now renamed "realism" and put on national television. So it is that adultery, fornication, wickedness, and all the other evils (by reason of which the judgment of God comes upon society) are practiced and promoted openly in our time. Modern television, often in the form of soap operas, is little more than the account of adulterous men and silly women laden with sin.

What a contrast virtue can present to this shameless generation. Indeed, the righteous Christian may be initially jeered at, but he is later to be respected. He will see virtue give credence to his testimony.

Why? Because eventually worldly pleasure comes to nothing. Soon the party is over, and the giddy, laughing young man and woman are alone in the darkness, smitten with a sense of the futility of it all. Millions in our world ask, Whom can I trust? What can I believe in? Where can I discover hope and a cleansing for my soul?

For an answer to this question, the sinner under conviction is not about to turn to drunken friends or stoned associates. Even he knows that the blind cannot lead the blind. He will turn to the believer whom he knows is going straight, who has not bowed the knee to Baal, Bacchus, or Eros. The credentials of virtue are the first requirement for a good witness for the Savior.

For spiritual success then, virtue is imperative. We must ask for God's help if we are to be delivered from the power of sin to the power of righteousness.

What is the power of righteousness? Great is the promise made to the Christian in this regard. The apostle Paul said, "For the law of the Spirit of life in Christ Jesus hath made me free from the law of sin and death. For what the law could not do, in that it was weak through the flesh, God sending his own Son in the likeness of sinful flesh, and for sin, condemned sin in the flesh: that the righteousness of the law might be fulfilled in us, who walk not after the flesh, but after the Spirit" (Romans 8:2-4).

The promise? It is that a new law of righteousness works mightily within us called "the law of the spirit of life in Christ Jesus." God has, therefore, promised His mighty working within the very being of all who trust in Him. The Christian is, indeed, "married to another," not the old law but a new partner, that he might bring forth the fruit of righteousness unto God.

There's another source of help in the pursuit of virtue.

In addition to his earnest prayer for divine help, the concerned Christian should daily read the Word of God for the righteous strength it builds within the soul. Along with studying the Word, he should nobly purpose that he will obey the Word, saying yes to God and no to the devil every day that he lives. In this regard, he is wonderfully promised that sin no longer has dominion over him in that he is not under law but under grace. Sin has been defeated for us by the Captain of our salvation.

However, many say, "But I have sinned." Even as Christians our most pressing question may be, "How is virtue restored?" What if we fail in the practice of virtue? It is possible for a Christian to commit sins contrary to the righteous law within his own heart. Obviously it is. Many have. How then is virtue restored? How is moral capability returned to the life of one who, even though a Christian, has transgressed the moral will of God? Is there forgiveness, cleansing, and restoration for the erring child of the King?

We have a welcome promise concerning this pressing question in the Word of God. To every convicted believer the Bible says, "If we confess our sins, he is faithful and just to forgive us our sins, and to cleanse us from all unrighteousness" (1 John 1:9).

What a grand provision! Fellowship with God and spiritual capability can be restored in the life of the believer on the basis of his confession and divine forgiveness. Indeed, we may well need to often ask for forgiveness and cleansing in our walk with God. A righteous

God stands ready to forgive again on the basis of the shed blood of Jesus Christ.

David knew this. He was called a man after God's own heart. We know, however, that he committed the sins of adultery and then murder. He had other shortcomings, but still the Lord declared him righteous by imputed righteousness and a man after His own heart. Why? It was not because David's actions were perfect; it was because he knew where forgiveness came from. It came from God and was given to a humble heart that would confess its sin, its need, and petition for forgiveness.

Consider for a moment the results of a life of virtue. Every believer in pursuit of goodness would do well to read Proverbs 31. Here the question is posed: "Who can find a virtuous woman? For her price is far above rubies" (v. 10).

With compliment after compliment to such a person, the Lord tells us of the fruits of virtue in this gracious woman. Her husband safely trusts in her, she provides wonderful food and clothing for her family, she dependably carries out the business transactions of the family, she does not fear future calamity, her husband becomes a well-known leader, and she herself is wise and kind. Finally, her children rise up to call her blessed, and her husband lifts his praise of her.

Is the pursuit of virtue a costly, troublesome, vain, profitless endeavor? No, indeed! The opposite is true. The life of "easy virtue" is always a deteriorating one. It is only easy at the beginning and becomes painfully hard at the end. It leads its victims down into shame and rejection. It produces physical debilitation, mental deterioration, and, finally, spiritual disaster. It ultimately brings its chained and spiritless prisoners to the steps that lead down to hell. The simple equation is: virtue pays; vice does not.

Our society has yet to learn this lesson and probably never will before Christ comes again. The men and women of this world, following that familiar path of easy virtue, smile sweetly and approvingly at one another as they dance down the slippery slope to the grave.

Virtue is the answer to that often-repeated question, How can I be happy? In our world, promoters press the foolish answer that happiness comes from possessions, amusement, travel, indulgence, and other supposedly self-fulfilling activities. Our world has invented its own futile merry-go-round in the pursuit of happiness.

We will never find genuine happiness until we learn the connection between virtue and happiness. Happiness without virtue is an impossibility.

The person who gains riches at the sacrifice of virtue will find his riches to be impediments. A house filled with possessions gained by dishonesty will become a household of sorrows. To sacrifice virtue for something else is to give real gold in exchange for counterfeit. We see those in pursuit of that foolish course disintegrating before our very eyes. Our society has become plagued by AIDS, venereal disease, suicide, and evils of all kinds in the pursuit of happiness without virtue.

The call to virtue, to public righteousness, has moved up the scale of importance in our day. Virtue has never been an option, but in today's world it is becoming an essential to survival. The very fate of a nation could depend upon the practice of virtue.

God has said, "Righteousness exalteth a nation: but sin is a reproach to any people" (Proverbs 14:34). This principle applies to any nation and any people. Sin brings reproach, destroys reputations, erodes a nation's human potential, and can even bring a great culture to an end. Our present society is filled with illustrations of the connection between virtue and survival itself.

The current AIDS epidemic shouts this to all who will listen. Medical authorities now warn that hundreds of thousands per year may soon be dying from this pestilence that is fast becoming the curse of humanity. It has been called "the medical equivalent of nuclear holocaust." If left unabated, it could threaten the survival of the human race. Iniquity can become a reproach to any nation.

Whatever else AIDS is, it is a contagious disease that spreads largely through immoral activity. There are exceptions, of course, but for the majority, escape will be possible only for those who recognize that, in this case, virtue and survival are the same things.

The growing problem of drug addiction illustrates the same point. Traffic in illegal drugs has passed the $80 billion-a-year mark in the United States alone. Additional billions of dollars worth of these deadly, addictive substances are being sold to young people every day across the world. As many of these are added to cemetery populations, we have further proof that virtue and survival go hand in hand.

Nearly every critical issue of our world today is a connected to a problem of morality. The ultimately critical issue is the erosion of public morality. In this gross and insensate world, the maiden of virtue is being daily throttled by the ogre of vice. What's more, this brutalization is being done to the cheers, applause, promotion, and sponsorship of a major segment of our population. The masses of earth that formerly could be called by the name *humanity* is now changing fast. People are becoming brute beasts, made to be taken and destroyed.

In a thousand ways we see this. In our time we have seen statesmanship become politics, music become noise, enthusiasm become cynicism, love become sex, and sex become sodomy.

The deterioration is so apparent that even some of the cynical are calling for a return to morals and ethics. They dimly remember that there used to be something called "moral principles," and they wonder where to recover them. Within the heart of mankind, the awareness of the fact that there is a difference between right and wrong remains.

Western culture remembers enough about Christianity to feel guilt but not enough to know where forgiveness comes from. It remembers the need for virtue but does not remember Calvary—the only place where empowerment for virtue is found. Forgetting its Christian heritage, the West now thrashes about in an illness that could be terminal but that could be readily cured by the forgiving, cleansing, empowering blood of Jesus Christ.

The church of Jesus Christ is the custodian of a precious commodity. Knowing the source of virtue, it alone can properly relay that message to a needy world. Christ is the hope of all mankind; the Christian is to be the embodiment of that hope. The believer who will add virtue to his faith will become the kind of person that the world cannot do without.

Called by God to the path of virtue, let us begin on that path today. One good thing done today may lead to two tomorrow. That may lead to four the next day, and then on to the exponential expansion of goodness in our lives. Virtue is, of course, its own reward. But, in addition, it will produce rich rewards when we stand approved in the shining presence of the One who has loved righteousness and hated iniquity. Virtue brings a bit of heaven to the heart here and much more of it when we arrive on that celestial shore.

Knowledge

4

The Imperative of Knowledge

Faith is the beginning of spiritual success. Once we have begun in faith, we need virtue to establish the moral direction of our lives. Unless that direction is established, what we do will be of little consequence. Our greatest efforts, finest plans, and noblest aspirations will be exercises in futility until we establish our moral direction. We must say, "God helping me, I will walk worthy of my high calling." We must add to our faith virtue.

Now Peter calls us to the next imperative—knowledge. Earlier in his letter, Peter congratulated his readers because they had received the gift of eternal life "through the knowledge of him," that is, Jesus Christ (2 Peter 1:3). Here he commends them for having the kind of knowledge imperative to salvation itself. When talking of this knowledge, Peter uses the word *epignosis*, which means "full knowledge." In the "full knowledge" of Christ, we have received His gift of eternal life. We have full and free salvation.

So thrilling is the possession of the full knowledge that produces salvation that Peter takes another moment to expand on it. The knowledge of Christ, he says, will bring us "all things that pertain unto life and godliness" (2 Peter 1:3). When one has Christ he has it all!

Later, when Peter tells us to expand our knowledge as Christians, he uses a different form of this word. Up to this point, however, he uses the word in the sense of "knowledge to which nothing can be added"—knowledge that is complete, perfect, full.

This definition of knowledge stands in contrast to a doctrine that has gained currency in our time. It is the notion that an experience subsequent to salvation is needed to bring us the "full salvation" we did not have, or had only partially, when we were saved. The teaching suggests that there is some qualitatively different form of the Christian life, sometimes called deeper, wider, fuller, or another qualifying name. This suggests that God reserves a qualitatively different form of life for the deeper Christian.

Indeed, there are a hundred names for this position in Christendom, and we can be sure that new ones will continue to be invented. Often they are presented to the inquirer by someone who professes to have discovered "the blessed secret" or some other hidden knowledge. These previously undisclosed spiritual secrets are presented to the current generation of Christians as something new that was unknown and even unsuspected in the past.

Such assertions to mystical forms of knowledge are to be avoided. They tend to be more cultic than Christian. First, they are without basis in Scripture. Indeed, Scripture teaches that when we are saved by faith in Jesus Christ we are, at the same time, "blessed . . . with all spiritual blessings in heavenly places in Christ" (Ephesians

1:3). Therefore, we are complete in Him in whom dwells all the fullness of the Godhead bodily (Colossians 2:9).

In Scripture the essence of Christianity is described as "Christ in you, the hope of glory" (Colossians 1:27). Christ in me is not only all that I need, but He is all that there is.

In the full knowledge of Christ, we have complete, full salvation. To this salvation there is nothing to be added. Eternal life is assuredly mine because of "Christ in me." Fears of incompleteness are, therefore, unfounded. They will produce only unending confusion and frustration for the seeker. Believers who succumb to such teaching join those who are ever seeking and never coming to the knowledge of the truth.

How different it is for the true Christian. Knowing Christ, he rests in full salvation. But now, having congratulated us on this knowledge to which we cannot add, Peter still advises us to add knowledge to our faith and virtue. Here he uses the word gnōsis. This means knowledge that is not necessarily complete. It is growing knowledge. "Keep thinking," he in effect says. "Keep studying. Stimulate those intellectual appetites. You have a brain; use it!"

The intellectual life of the Christian requires more thought than we may give it. There remains an excessive amount of what might be called wrong-headedness among believers concerning the place of intellect and the proper source of knowledge.

On one side, there is mere intellectualism. Many Christians, especially those saved in middle life, confess to having had excessive confidence in human knowledge. Intellectualism is the common faith of the unregenerate man. Having only the intelligence of this world, he trusts too much in human knowledge. He believes that science is the custodian of final truth and is to be trusted fully.

Those who tend to overly trust intellectualism need to learn again the limitations of knowledge. No one in this world knows the ultimate nature of things. We do not know what time is, what electricity is, what light is, what the essential building blocks of matter are, or what life itself is. No one knows why we wake up in the morning after sleeping or how the mind, which is immaterial, influences the body, which is material. We actually know—in a human sense—only pitifully few things. Beyond that, we know nothing. One who places his ultimate trust in human knowledge is sadly deceived. Every automobile accident, every psychiatric clinic, every cemetery demonstrates that the human brain, with its "natural" thought processes, is neither infallible nor eternal.

On the other side, some Christians maintain an attitude of extreme anti-intellectualism. They oppose all rational thinking or anything that bears the name *intellectual*. These unfortunate people have rejected study, schooling, and serious thinking as being nearly un-Christian. Too often they live their lives on a relatively small number of simple propositions and may even be susceptible to exploitation by a messianic leader. Such people often have no intellectual, rational defense against heresy, false doctrine, spiritual subversion, or other forms of cultic influence. They may go so far as to become snake handlers, poison takers, book burners, or pursuers of other forms of foolishness. Being anti-intellectual, they are drawn into a thoughtless form of biblical interpretation.

Similar mistaken theologies are produced by those who invent substitutes for real knowledge. These can include "great" experiences, ecstatic emotional involvements, unforgettable visions, voices in the night, or other subjective notions. Those who subscribe to such things resent the rigorous call in the Scripture to "prove all things" (1 Thessalonians 5:21) or to be sure that everything is established in the mouth of two or three witnesses (2 Corinthians 13:1). For many of them, even the authority of Scripture is relegated to a position inferior to "what God told me last night."

So we see that an anti-intellectual attitude is full of spiritual danger. Of course, all believers are not called upon or equipped to become theologians, but all are called upon to read, to study, and to know the Word. Each believer must consider the Word so as to become a dependable interpreter and communicator of Scripture, even to the extent that he is able to teach others. To the extent of our ability, we are to become intellectual participants in the battle for truth.

We are to add to our virtue knowledge. Where, then, do we find this knowledge?

Certainly, above all other sources available, we must look to the source of sources—the sacred pages of Scripture. Here we have available to us the Word of the living and true God. Here, in these sacred pages, God has given us the greatest of all treasure houses of wisdom. Not to avail ourselves of that wisdom is to deny ourselves a necessary component of spiritual success and to assure that we shall live in intellectual poverty.

A student in the Word is pursuing life's most profitable activity. The new Christian does well to enroll in a carefully structured study program. He should learn the books of the Bible and their major themes. He should quickly grasp the great doctrines of the Scripture and answers to the basic questions. These include, Who is God? What is man? What is sin? What is the way of salvation?

Structured study is foundational to knowledge. No Christian is mature until he has learned to study the Bible for himself and can trust his conclusions. The individual must come to the place where he can read, know, and be confident of his own convictions concerning the Word of God. He must become a student of the Word, not merely a follower of someone else's teaching.

In fact, genuine progress in the church and its call to evangelize the world will not be made short of this. Teachers and leaders must not aspire to simply gain disciples for themselves and with them construct a kingdom. Rather, they must produce students who will themselves become teachers and produce other students who will teach others also. As knowledge is given to us in ever-increasing measure, we are to become teachers of the Word (Hebrews 5:12).

Second to learning from the study of the Word itself is careful attention to biblical preaching.

The preached Word brings an additional source of spiritual profit. Preaching is a combination of teaching, illustration, application, admonition, encouragement, and hearing. Happy is the Christian who has the regular opportunity to hear good expository preaching. People and nations have been lifted from danger, poverty, and despair by the powerful preaching of the Word of God.

Some may say, "My pastor does not preach like that." All who lift a voice from the pulpit should aspire to be powerful and effective voices for the Lord. But, of course, some are not. How can I derive blessing from their preaching? This is where personal Bible knowledge comes to the fore. We need to know how to *listen* to a sermon.

Listening to any sermon with profit is easy if done while keeping our knowledge of the Word in mind. If the message is doctrinally unsound, we should ask, What is the precise truth of Scripture concerning this matter? If a verse is misquoted, quote the correct verse to yourself. If an illustration does not illustrate—and a few do not—then think of one that does.

A personal reservoir of biblical and world knowledge becomes the data against which we can measure each message. It is difficult for one with no basic knowledge to add to his knowledge. Conversely, the knowledgeable mind can multiply its knowledge with every new thought that comes. "Unto every one that hath shall be given" is certainly true. Conversely, "from him that hath not shall be taken away even that which he hath" (Matthew 25:29). In few ways is this more applicable than in the pursuit of knowledge. A small improvement can be multiplied into a great gain; the near empty mind is difficult to teach at all.

Additional knowledge comes to us through the practice of reflective thinking. Facts are rarely usable until they have been made to fit the truths already there. Reflective thinking is a constant process. We hear something and find ourselves saying, "That just *cannot* be true." Then we hear a fact that instantly rings true, and we grasp it immediately and insert it into the puzzle of life. Adding new pieces to the puzzle is what education is all about. No number of facts will produce this result. One who does not discriminate between various sources of information is intellectually lazy and will be forever naive.

The call to reflective thinking is extended to us in the Word. Paul wrote to the church at Philippi and admonished them to live above anxiety, promising the peace of God as the alternative to worry and frustration. What is the key to avoiding that frustration? Is there a course we can take in pursuit of the high road? The answer is yes.

We find the key to that pursuit in these words: "Finally, brethren, whatsoever things are true, whatsoever things are honest, whatsoever things are just, whatsoever things are pure, whatsoever things are lovely, whatsoever things are of good report; if there be any virtue, and if there be any praise, think on these things. Those things, which ye have both learned, and received, and heard, and seen in me, do: and the God of peace shall be with you" (Philippians 4:8-9).

Paul lays out a program that can be both therapeutic and sustaining. The believer can ask himself daily, *Have I thought today on the things that are true, honest, just, pure, lovely, virtuous, praiseworthy, and of encouraging report?* A mind filled with these things cannot go far wrong. It is well known that we tend to become like the object of our contemplation. Contemplation on these virtues must inevitably make our lives things of quality as well.

Great books are another source of knowledge. The best of them should be read—some more than once. If you have never walked through the wicket gate in *Pilgrim's Progress,* you have deprived yourself of a rewarding experience. Augustine's *City of God* still has much to say to Christians today. Kempis's *The Imitation of Christ* provides an applicable pattern for our lives. No one should miss *Mere Christianity* by C. S. Lewis, who has also given us *The Screwtape Letters.*

"Give attendance to reading," Paul said to Timothy (1 Timothy 4:13). That call has never been easier to fulfill. In Paul's day, written material was available only on parchments that were rare, expensive, and easily ruined. Reading was counted a great privilege reserved for the few. Now the church library, the Christian bookstore, the public library, even the doctor's office can become a fountain of knowledge. Wisdom cries in the streets.

In our quest we must not disregard another possible source of knowledge—one that is, perhaps, more readily available than any other. It is intelligent conversation. Intelligent conversation is free, it is fascinating, it is food for the soul and fine tuning for the fertile mind. The interaction between two intelligent Christian minds going in the same direction is one of life's most precious gifts.

Where do we find such conversation? Simple. Begin with someone who knows something, and ask him what he knows. Articulate people everywhere can provide us with a trove of knowledge. We do well never to let such a person get away without first giving us a thought we can keep.

Considering the possibilities, it is unfortunate that so many of our conversations degenerate into discussions of unworthy, banal things. What a tragedy that when people eat together, they talk about the food. How sad that the weather or the decor should sustain so many conversations, supplanting the treasures of the mind. The quality of life for individuals, families, the church, the community would be lifted if our conversation were to improve —even a little.

Remember that good, stimulating conversation is a two-way street. Proper conversations do not consist of one always asking questions and the other always answering. Each of us must bring some contribution. That is not as difficult as it may sound. Each of us knows some facts that are unique to us. We can memorize a little poetry, read an unknown book, check some data that might not be generally known. Possessing that, we will become a valued member of any circle of intelligent and stimulating conversation. Pursuing this course, any one of us can be a source of spiritual profit to ourselves and others. The principle of Scripture that says, "Give, and it shall be given unto you" (Luke 6:38), applies to more than just the coin of the realm. Give of yourself, of the best thoughts of your mind, and the results will be to your spiritual profit.

Intelligent Christian conversation has the potential to benefit us all.

Why is that? Because words are real things. Thoughts are close to the ultimate substance of life. Wealthy is the person who keeps his thoughts on a high level and who possesses an adequate reservoir of words with which to express them. Such riches can be given away without having their value diminished.

The modern media has helped contribute to the impoverishment of thought in our society. Television, radio, and print offer us a combined daily fare that is predigested and tasteless. Flashing pictures and meaningless slogans have taken the place of rich conversation and good thinking in our time. In defense, Christians need to form groups that simply get together to think and to talk to one another about the good things of the Lord and of the Word. Failing that, we may soon be without the sound biblical knowledge we need to survive in this world. Thomas Jefferson touched on a similar theme when he said, "If a nation expects to be ignorant and free, in a state of civilization, it expects what never was and never shall be." The same can be said about the church. The individual or group that does not seek to expand its knowledge will soon be controlled by others.

Scripture calls us to obtain yet another aspect of knowledge. It is the knowledge of God's will. The apostle Paul said, "Be ye not unwise, but understanding what the will of the Lord is" (Ephesians 5:17). Knowledge of God's will gives us spiritual purpose. Without that knowledge our lives will be aimless and meaningless. Unfortunately, even within the Body of Christ, too many believers are milling about, buttonholing others, asking the old questions, reciting the slogans, and hesitating to move. For lack of knowledge, their lives are impotent.

In fact, in admonishing us to be knowledgeable, Paul said, "Be not unwise." He used a strong Greek word that can be translated "mindless." By this, Paul implied that the one who does not know the will of God is, in fact, without a mind. We can be sure that the purpose of our ability is to know and do the will of God. Knowledge is not merely the accumulation of a set of facts, but it is the ingestion of the data that it takes to know and then to do the will of God.

The pursuit of this kind of knowledge should be an ever-growing thing. Our awareness of the purpose of God and our moving toward that purpose each day—this is spiritual maturity. It is time for many believers to stop and ask themselves, *Having learned what I have learned, experienced what I have experienced, and now knowing what I know, what purpose will I accomplish for Christ?* No matter how brilliant a believer may be, he may just as well be ignorant if he has not forced himself to ask and to properly answer this question.

We are to gain knowledge for a purpose, not merely so that we may have clever answers to things practical, prophetic, or profound. Knowledge, like all other things, must never be sought for its own sake. It must be pursued for the sake of Christ, for the sake of spiritual accomplishment. Our growing knowledge, to be valid, must be translated into spiritual activity. God calls us to know and then to do.

Few principles can be more valuably emphasized in life. In this day of wide dissemination of facts concerning Christianity, many believers have developed a commendable repository of knowledge. Such knowledge is a valuable asset. However, there comes a time when the asset turns into a liability. Knowledge, even biblical knowledge, can cause us to be proud, puffed up, and unduly impressed with ourselves. We can spend our time arguing about the fine points rather than witnessing to the faith of the gospel. Warning us repeatedly of this danger, the Bible insists that we are to be not only hearers of the Word but doers also (James 1:22). One who hears, who becomes knowledgeable, but does not share his knowledge is risking spiritual stagnation.

We are told in the Word that to whom much has been given, much shall be required. True about many things, this principle is eminently true about the possession of knowledge. To possess knowledge is to possess responsibility to bring that knowledge to those ignorant of the Word of God and of the message of salvation.

There is enough knowledge in any Christian community to turn that community into an explosive entity, a witness for Christ to the whole world. The Christian community that has knowledge but does not take it to the world is also risking spiritual stagnation. And who can doubt that evidence of spiritual stagnation is in the Body of Christ in our time?

To faith and virtue we must add knowledge. Having added that knowledge, we must pray that it will guide us to new accomplishments for Christ.

Knowledge is essential for many reasons. More than ever, it is essential in helping us avoid the spiritual subversion that is coming upon the church with tremendous force in these last days. The church is being bombarded with mounting waves of unsound doctrine, bad theology, cultic views, occult practices, and human philosophies. The Christian community must heed the warnings of Scripture and diligently pursue the knowledge that can protect it from spiritual subversion. Throughout church history, the enemy has lurked in the shadows at the edge of the lighted circle that is Christianity, ready to steal the young, weak, and ignorant away from Christ.

That happened in Galatia. Paul had just conducted an effective mission there, preaching the wonder of salvation by grace. The people were so impressed with his message that they would have plucked out their eyes and given them to him in gratefulness for the deliverance from sin and the law.

The evangelistic party led by Paul had hardly left town, however, when the Judaizers came with their program of spiritual subversion. They preached that grace was fine but that ultimate justification required the observance of the law of Moses. They began to subvert these still-ignorant Christians.

Upon hearing this, Paul wrote with concern:

> I marvel that ye are so soon removed from him that called you into the grace of Christ unto another gospel: which is not another; but there be some that trouble you, and would pervert the gospel of Christ. But though we, or an angel from heaven, preach any other gospel unto you than that which we have preached unto you, let him be accursed. As we said before, so say I now again, if any man preach any other gospel unto you than that ye have received, let him be accursed. (Galatians 1:6-9)

In their ignorance, the Galatians were vulnerable to spiritual subversion. They were vulnerable because they did not know and obey the truth. They did not know that in the knowledge of Christ they had received all that pertains to life and godliness. Out of ignorance, they became vulnerable to the offer of "something more."

Our need to understand Scripture and practice sound doctrine becomes more apparent as we move toward the end of the age. We are warned that new forms of spiritual subversion will come upon believers in the latter days: "Now the Spirit speaketh expressly, that in the latter times some shall depart from the faith, giving heed to seducing spirits, and doctrines of devils" (1 Timothy 4:1). Believers untutored in sound doctrine will be vulnerable to the point of giving heed to doctrines of demons. We can be sure that Satan will promote his lies more forcefully when he has the opportunity.

Many of us are surprised at the bizarre doctrines and preposterous promises of modern religionists. I am more surprised at the thousands—even millions—of people who have no more sense than to buy into their package—at a price, of course. For want of knowledge, people are allowing false teachers to deceive and exploit them. They are unable to discern between lies and hypocrisy and truth.

We need a revival of knowledge to save us from Satan's lies. The pursuit of knowledge is not an extravagance—it is one of the keys to spiritual survival and success.

Self-Control

5

The Imperative of Self-Control

As we grow in the Christian life, our responsibility grows. If we ever had a call to personal responsibility, we have it in the next imperative.

It is the Greek word *enkrateia*. At its root is the word *kratos*, which is one of the words used in Scripture for "power" or "strength." The word occurs four times in the New Testament and is each time rendered "temperance" in the King James Version. It does, however, mean more than that. Vine comments that " 'self-control' is the preferable rendering, as temperance is now limited to but one form of self-control; the various powers bestowed by God upon man are capable of abuse; the right use demands the controlling power of the will under the operation of the Spirit of God; in Acts 24:25, the word follows 'righteousness,' which represents God's claims, self-control being man's response thereto; in 2 Peter 1:6, it follows 'knowledge,' suggesting that what is learnt requires to be put into practice."

Let us expand upon those thoughts. In his letter to the believers at Ephesus, Paul opens by announcing his love and faithful concern for them. He said, "Wherefore I also, after I heard of your faith in the Lord Jesus, and love unto all the saints, cease not to give thanks for you, making mention of you in my prayers, that the God of our Lord Jesus Christ, the Father of glory, may give unto you the spirit of wisdom and revelation in the knowledge of him: the eyes of your understanding being enlightened; that ye may know what is the hope of his calling, and what the riches of the glory of his inheritance in the saints, and what is the exceeding greatness of his power to usward who believe, according to the working of his mighty power, which he wrought in Christ, when he raised him from the dead" (Ephesians 1:15-20). When referring to the exceeding greatness of the power of Christ, Paul uses the word *kratos*. By this, he is referring to the power that God exercises, guaranteeing the stability of His universe. The meaning of the word comes close to "sovereignty" or "stability."

Paul is praying that each of these believers will exercise sovereignty over the affairs of their lives and will have the power to control and stabilize their lives in much the same way that God controls the universe.

We also find an interesting contrast to this idea in Scripture. Paul tells Timothy in the third chapter of his second epistle to him that perilous times shall come in the last days. He gives a list of reasons for these perilous times: "For men shall be lovers of their own selves, covetous, boasters, proud, blasphemers, disobedient to parents, unthankful, unholy, without natural affection, trucebreakers, false accusers, *incontinent*, fierce, despisers of those that are good, traitors, heady, high-minded, lovers of pleasures more than lovers of God" (2 Timothy 3:2-3, emphasis added).

Here we have a list of the attitudes that will characterize sinners at the end of the age. One of them is distinguished by the word *incontinent*. In English this word means "unable to contain oneself," "the absence of self-control," or "out of control." In the original language, the word is *akratos*.

Note that to be incontinent is the opposite of being stable or of exercising self-control. The same root is used in both of these instances, but one means self-control and the other means the absence of self-control. The call to self-control, to personal stability, to the exercise of personal responsibility, is one of the imperatives of the successful Christian life.

The Christian is responsible to control himself. Instructed by the Word of God, enlightened by the Spirit of God, we are to live responsibly for Christ. By so doing, we will pursue a course of minimal frustration and of maximum blessing. The challenge of the Christian life is responsible living. Self-control can bring stability to the individual, the family, and the nation.

The stable, self-controlled life of the Christian provides a contrast to the erratic, unstable age in which we live. As we approach the consummation of history, we see emotional and spiritual instability taking over the hearts of men. The unsettled nature of our time becomes obvious as we see men and women lose the willingness and then the ability to control themselves.

Governments and their leaders have become unstable for want of self-control. Erosion of leadership will produce further instability, even anarchy, in society. The hearts of men fail them as they visualize a nation out of control. In Scripture, the disappearance of strong, stable leaders in a society is a sign that the Lord is withdrawing His hand of blessing and direction.

To the nation of Israel, God said, "For, behold, the Lord, the Lord of hosts, doth take away from Jerusalem and from Judea the stay and the staff, the whole stay of bread, and the whole stay of water, the mighty man, and the man of war, the judge, and the prophet, and the prudent, and the ancient, the captain of fifty, and the honourable man, and the counsellor, and the cunning artificer, and the eloquent orator. And I will give children to be their princes, and babes shall rule over them. . . . As for my people, children are their oppressors, and women rule over them" (Isaiah 3:1-4, 12).

Let us consider some other signs of our times. The world economy is becoming increasingly unstable. We used to think of banks, lending institutions, and even our government as reliable, rock-like entities that brought stability to a fluid society. But that is no longer the case. The governments of the world owe trillions of dollars, and banks are failing at an ever-mounting rate. We see in Scripture that economic instability will grow toward the end of the age, eventually producing poverty, famine, and despair (Revelation 6:5-6).

Religious thinking has become more unstabilized. Modern theology has gone from liberalism to neo-orthodoxy to "God-is-dead" theology to liberation theology in a short time. New religious fads and quasi-theologies have taken root, and they continue to change month by month. Religious thought has always been changing, but it is now changing faster than ever. "Whom can I trust?" says the man of the world. The answer must come from the lips and the lives of true believers.

The call to self-control reminds us of the nature of our relationship to God. Knowing that God is all-powerful and man finite, we might imagine that the obedient Christian becomes little more than a marionette, his arms and legs activated by strings from heaven and controlled by an unseen hand.

But the call to self-control defeats that notion. The believer conducts his life on the basis of instructions from the Lord, but he is not a thoughtless, unwilling puppet. The plan of God is accomplished in our world by the will of the believer responding affirmatively to the will of God as given in the Word. To say that the Holy Spirit controls us is a less-than-accurate description of the relationship between the believer and his Lord. It is rather true that He instructs us, He leads us, and we, by doing the will of God, perform heaven's purposes.

The call is not for the believer to abandon himself to God. Rather he is called to responsible, thoughtful, willful obedience. Our commitment to Christ should not be presented as self-abandonment but self-control. We are not called to surrender ourselves to Him. Rather, we are "labourers together with God" (1 Corinthians 3:9). This call to commitment in Christ is expressed in Scripture by the word *present* (Romans 12:1) and the word *yield* (Romans 6:13). Both of these ideas find their source in the Greek word *paraistimi*.

This fascinating compound word literally means "stand up next to God." Its origin is interesting. In the course of battle, a commander would give careful instructions to the officers responsible for commanding the troops. After laying out the battle plan, he would ask them two questions: "Do you understand the order of the battle?" and, "Do you commit yourself as a responsible lieutenant commander?" If the answer was affirmative on both counts, the lieutenant saluted and said, "Yes, sir!"

In like fashion, each of us must ask himself, *Do I understand the will of the great Commander? Do I commit myself to courageously perform my responsibilities in the great battle?* If your answer is yes on both counts, you are invited to participate as a responsible individual in fulfilling heaven's program in this world.

To understand this is to see the significance of the call to self-control. God is not a puppeteer; He is a father!

He is raising responsible sons. He refuses to provide us with easy deliverance from the problems of life. He does not protect us from the buffeting storms that cause us to grow. He does not send a miracle in response to our every prayer. He withdraws His hand so that we might be more resourceful, more responsible, in facing the problems of life.

Contrary to the thinking of some modern preaching, the larger our problems, the greater the responsibility entrusted to us. The evidence of the gracious working of God in our lives is not health, wealth, comfort, flower-strewn pathways, and an effortless existence. Such a life produces weakness, ineffectiveness, irresponsibility, immorality, and ultimate failure. To promise such a pathetic, meaningless existence as the result of faith is to promise the unscriptural and the absurd.

It is the converse of this that is true. To promise the opportunity to suffer for Christ, to bear the cross, to labor unrewarded, to live dangerously, and to perhaps die gloriously for the Savior is to promise the truth. All of these things are part of the great adventure of living for our wonderful Lord.

Let no one resent the call to strength, to personal responsibility, to self-control, to temperance, to careful living. Do not let the call to prosperity lure you into the expectation of easy victories. Strong sons of God are not perfected by childish pursuits. "You are responsible," is what the Bible teaches. "Exercise self-discipline in order to gain the skill and the strength to be a good soldier, following divine instructions." Let us, then, no longer blame God for failures produced by folly or irresponsibility on our part.

We must pray that God will give us the ability to be strong, purposeful, and self-controlled. We need such people, responsible and strong children of God, because it is the destiny of redeemed man to rule the universe. The apostle Paul makes this remarkable promise clear in saying, "If we suffer [with Christ], we shall also reign with him" (2 Timothy 2:12). Man has been chosen by God to share in the rulership of the eternal worlds to come. The Christian life does not exist only for the moment; it is the prelude to glorious and eternal responsibilities.

We are called to live responsibly in an unstable world. It became unstable the moment that man chose disobedience to God. As a result of one irresponsible decision, man turned over to Satan his own mandate to rule the world, given to him by God. Satan became the prince of this world and the ruler of this evil age.

God allows evil to continue—temporarily. He uses the instability it creates to produce strength and responsibility in man. When he comes to Christ, man is given the opportunity to retrieve that responsibility, that mastery of life, from the hands of Satan.

As you and I retrieve that responsibility, we can expect to be opposed on every hand. Satan will dog the footsteps of the sincere believer, attempting to force him to relinquish his responsibility to God. Satan will attempt to beguile the believer into submitting, even in a small way, once again to Satan's own leadership. To accomplish this, he will feed him believable lies and attractive alternatives to righteousness.

The Christian must steel himself against the blandishments of the evil one. He must heed the warning "Be sober, be vigilant; because your adversary the devil, as a roaring lion, walketh about, seeking whom he may devour" (1 Peter 5:8). Peter said, "Whom resist stedfast in the faith, knowing that the same afflictions are accomplished in your brethren that are in the world. But the God of all grace, who hath called us unto his eternal glory by Christ Jesus, after that ye have suffered a while, make you perfect, stablish, strengthen, settle you" (vv. 9-10).

The Christian who pursues this course will never again relinquish the leadership of his life to the devil but will retrieve from Satan the thing he has stolen—the opportunity for responsibility.

We have, in the Word of God, the call to self-control, to stability, to a level of responsibility lost to much of humanity. By these things the Christian can distinguish himself in time and gain the right to serve in eternity.

Self-control is nothing less than mastery of life. That mastery will ultimately bring us kingly, eternal responsibilities. The wise person labors to master his life at all costs. The cost of investment in a disciplined life is infinitely small in comparison to the rewards of that life. All for whom life is important must seek to answer the questions, "What does it take to achieve the mastery of life?" and, "How can I gain self-control?" Those who seek this life sincerely find themselves led by God, as a child by a father, from spiritual infancy to spiritual maturity, to a life characterized by self-control. What will the growing, maturing child of God learn?

He will learn, first of all, that mastery of life takes purity of purpose. Scripture says it is impossible to serve two masters. We cannot effectively serve Christ on the high road and harbor a secret agenda of selfish advantage or personal gain. Mastery of life comes to those who seek the kingdom of God first, last, and always. There must be no rationalizing, no allowance for exceptions, no yielding the control of our life to another. "Know ye not, that to whom ye yield yourselves servants to obey, his servants ye are to whom ye obey; whether of sin unto death, or of obedience unto righteousness?" (Romans 6:16) The believer who would be a good soldier in the army of righteousness is in a constant battle with sin.

Scripture never presents this as an easy course. It was not easy for Paul, who said, "For we know that the law is spiritual: but I am carnal, sold under sin. For that which I do I [understand] not: for what I would, that do I not; but what I hate, that do I. . . . For I know that in me, (that is, in my flesh,) dwelleth no good thing: for to will is present with me; but how to perform that which is good I find not. For the good that I would I do not: but the evil which I would not, that I do" (Romans 7:14-15, 18-19) Finally, Paul cried out, "Oh, wretched man that I am!" (v. 24).

To continue on the path of self-control, Paul had to come regularly before God for confession, forgiveness, and cleansing. The mastery of life will not come to the sluggard or to the proud. It is for the humble. Self-mastery takes motivation. If we are not motivated, sleep will become our master, ease will become our master, food will become our master, friends will become our master, or a thousand other things will master us. Our life will be dissipated in myriad directions for lack of motivation.

Where do we find such motivation? Obviously we do not find it in money. We do not find it in reputation or in human accomplishment. For Paul and for us, motivation comes when "the love of Christ constraineth us" (2 Corinthians 5:14). It is the love of Christ that will drive us out of bed in the morning and keep us going through the day, long after earthly motivations have been left behind. Without spiritual motivation our lives become aimless and purposeless. Love for Christ is the fuel that can propel our lives.

But once we have the power, we must move in the right direction. Paul said, "I press toward the mark for the prize of the high calling of God in Christ Jesus" (Philippians 3:14). He knew that to reach a goal you must have a target. We establish our direction by asking, "Where am I going? What am I doing? How far am I along?"

Self-control can be accomplished only when we are in motion toward our goal. If we are filled with purpose, motivated, and on the right road, we have to begin moving. Spiritual progress is something like riding a bicycle. A bicycle is impossible to balance when it is standing still. Forward motion is what makes riding it possible. Just so, on our spiritual journey, we have little need of high-quality fuel, power steering, accurate maps, and carefully set goals when we are at home asleep in our chairs. When we aren't moving we can detach our minds from our goals, and no one will be the wiser. However, nothing could be more dangerous than to stop concentrating when we are in a race.

The Christian in motion is the one who is mastering his life. Having mastered this life, he can look forward to the privilege and responsibility of exercising his gifts as a co-regent of the universe with his blessed Lord.

Patience

6

The Imperative of Patience

Everything does not run at the same speed. The airplane and the automobile, if starting out from the same place at the same time, are not likely to arrive at a given destination at the same moment.

By the same token, it is unlikely that any two people in the world move at the same speed. Neither do they have the same ideas, the same convictions, the same outlook, the same principles, or the same way of doing things. As there are no two leaves alike in the world, neither are there two identical people.

Nevertheless, it is necessary for people to work together. Diversity tends to produce disagreement, not only in the world but also in the ranks of believers. It is unlikely that we will find two believers of precisely the same frame of mind and degree of energy. In fact, we can be reasonably sure that if we find any two people doing something in harmony, they have probably been trained to work together and even to compensate for one another. Apart from this, perfectly coordinated activity—even among members of the Body of Christ—is rare.

What can compensate for diversity? What bridge can span the gulf between people who do not share an identical vision of the world or the Lord? Patience.

Here again we have an interesting Greek word (*hupomone*), which literally means "an abiding under" and is almost invariably translated into English as "patience."

Each believer will one day find himself under some pressure, some problem, some weight, some frustrating circumstance that cannot be changed. No Christian in this imperfect world has not been confronted with apparently unsolvable problems. Work as we will, hope as we will, pray as we will, the limitation or liability will not go away.

The retarded child does not improve. The chronic pain persists even after medication. The debt left from foolish economic decisions hangs like a persistent dark cloud. The wayward child continues to rebel. The rain that prevents the harvest continues to fall. The wheelchair of a loved one is not thrown away. The automobile wheezes and then stops a hundred miles short of its goal. The problems continue, and each solution seems to produce three new difficulties.

In the face of these things, what should we do? What should be our course of action? Sometimes we can do something. But sometimes—and perhaps more so as life goes on—no options remain.

For the resourceful people, the accomplishers, these roadblocks are particularly frustrating. As they moved at cruising speed through the mine fields of life, there was always a plan. If it failed, there was an alternate plan. If that failed, youth, health, money, or creativity made other options possible. Never did altitude and ideas run out at the same time. Whatever the problem, they overcame it and moved on.

There comes a time, however, when life turns out differently. In any circumstance, there are only a finite number of options and possibilities. When young, we mistakenly think of ourselves as packages of infinity for whom nothing is impossible. Eventually, however, we discover that the word *impossible* has real meaning. What then do we do? We have no choice but to exercise the fifth imperative—patience.

This is the time when we learn to live under that burden that will not go away. As patience matures, we learn not merely to endure but to appreciate the value of facing the unsolvable problem. To come to this place is to see fulfilled in our lives the admonition "Let patience have her perfect work" (James 1:4). Until we reach that point, Scripture tells us again and again, "You have need of patience."

Of course, some will deny this need. They may have built a system of theology that says that every problem can be solved instantly by a spiritual formula. They hold that God stands ready at all times to work a miracle for them so that every difficulty of life is soon dispelled.

This doctrine is one of Satan's lies, but it remains stubbornly with us despite the fact that it is contradicted both by the Bible and by the experience of those who live in a real world. Those who are most susceptible to the doctrine of instant deliverance often know little of the Word of God. They become easy prey for false teachers. Eventually, however, unsolved problems and seemingly unanswered prayers lead them to doubt. When they inquire of their spiritual mentors as to this lack of response from God, they are told, "You just don't have enough faith!" Those who hold this view of God are candidates for ultimate despair.

How much better to hope in the Lord and to let our prayers rest with Him. How much better to follow our greatest example, who said, "Not my will, but thine, be done" (Luke 22:42). How much better to labor in the cultivation of patience rather than presumption.

One of the most blessed Christian attitudes is that of hope. Hope causes us to anticipate each new day, saying, "Today my bright anticipations may be realized. If not today, then perhaps tomorrow. If not tomorrow, I will still hope in the Lord. I know that He has not forgotten, and that He stands ready in His perfect time to do His wonderful will for me." This attitude of hope is a joy to see in other people and a thrill to discover in our own lives.

The doctrine of instant fulfillment is the enemy of hope. Hope, combined with patience, keeps the heart filled with joyous anticipation, "For we are saved by hope: but hope that is seen is not hope: for what a man seeth, why doth he yet hope for? But if we hope for that we see not, then do we with patience wait for it" (Romans 8:24-25).

Each of us needs to hear the words "You have need of patience!" For each of us, there will be many times in which we are unable to work out our problems "without remainder." In a sinful world we will have instability and uncertainty. In the equation of life on earth, we cannot expect everything to come out balanced and even. Each day we will be called of God to exercise patience. How shall we do it? Is there a course of action we can follow to keep us sane in such a world? There certainly is!

To develop patience, we must remember that God's plan is better that ours. He knows, He understands, and He sees the end from the beginning. He is constantly working to produce for us a brighter design and a better destiny than any we can fashion in our constricted, little minds.

Have we not, in some measure, discovered this already? I can testify that virtually every one of my prayers has been or is in the process of being answered by two words from the Lord. Those words are *better* and *later*. "Better, but later." This is more than often the divine answer for me. I imagine that it is the same for most of us.

Better—more wonderful than anything we have dreamed—is the divine intention for us. Isn't it true that most of our deepest apprehensions never come to pass? Isn't it true that most of our prayers have been answered (excluding those that are not still in the process) by a working of God more marvelous than anything we expected?

We can rejoice over the fact that so many of our foolish, immature, demanding requests are denied by the Lord. If each of our prayers were answered instantly and precisely according to our demands, most of us would be in a horrible situation. We may have moved into the wrong profession, married the wrong man or woman, committed ourselves to the wrong principles, or done a thousand other foolish things. Would not our condition now be worse than hopeless if God had not required us to be patient rather than grant us each wish the first time we gave the prayer wheel a spin? God was waiting to do something better for us.

Biblical history yields many illustrations of prayers that were answered but that did not produce the results that the impatient prayer had in mind. Remember the admonition to be careful for what we pray, because God may answer our prayers.

The prayer of Hezekiah is a good example of this principle at work. "In those days was Hezekiah sick unto death. And the prophet Isaiah the son of Amoz came to him, and said unto him, Thus saith the Lord, Set thine house in order; for thou shalt die, and not live. Then he turned his face to the wall, and prayed unto the Lord" (2 Kings 20:1-2).

Hezekiah earnestly besought the Lord to let him live. He told the Lord he had walked in truth before Him with a perfect heart and had done much that was good in the sight of the Lord. After that, Hezekiah wept before God.

As a result of this prayer, God sent the prophet Isaiah to tell Hezekiah that his prayer was heard and his tears were seen. God healed Hezekiah and promised to restore his life for fifteen more years. Hezekiah even asked God for a sign that the prayer was answered. God caused the sundial to go backward ten degrees. What a sign of answered prayer!

But what were the results of this answered prayer? The result was that Hezekiah, in this extended period of his life, betrayed the will of God and allowed the representatives from the evil kingdom of Babylon to see all of the precious treasures in the house of the Lord. Because of this, Isaiah told him of the judgment of God that would come upon the house of Hezekiah, "Behold, the days come, that all that is in thine house, and that which thy fathers have laid up in store unto this day, shall be carried into Babylon: nothing shall be left, saith the Lord" (v. 17). Isaiah also gave Hezekiah the dreadful news that Hezekiah's own sons would become eunuchs in the palace of the king of Babylon (v. 18).

The invasion and capture of Jerusalem by the king of Babylon began the times of the Gentiles, a drastic watershed in history. This and many other evils came out of the extended life of King Hezekiah.

Is it true that answered prayers are always the best thing? Can it be demonstrated that, when God answers prayer, the results will always be happy? Reading the dramatic account of Hezekiah should give us a warning. Someone has said, "More tears are shed over answered prayers than over unanswered prayers by far." If Hezekiah had died, he would have gone into eternity a faithful servant of God. The extension of his life brought a blight on his record. By faith, we must believe that God may have something better for us than the thing for which we ask.

God may also elect to answer our prayers later than we expect. Scripture promises that "all things work together for good to them that love God" (Romans 8:28). That implies that God has a time process in mind. Later is often better. Many of the things for which we pray are probably bigger, more demanding, or more dangerous than we can handle at the time. To learn patience, remember that God has a better—and often later—plan.

Patience also comes in remembering that we are not God. We are simply not in a position to pound the table before the throne of our heavenly Father and demand that we hear from Him now—"or else!" Or else what? Nothing. Having presented our requests to God, we have no recourse but to see what God may do at whatever time He elects to do it.

But there is a secret to patience worth noting. The secret is to do something else in the meantime. For those of us who are not omniscient, a plan is desirable, but an alternate plan is almost always necessary. With an alternative in mind, whatever is still usable when the first plan fails can be used in the second plan, which still may succeed.

Napoleon Bonaparte was one of the great military geniuses—perhaps the greatest in history. He won every battle he fought, except the last one. On forty occasions he was able to triumph over foes who were often superior in number and firepower. One of his methods was that of the alternate plan. During battle, he had an alternative ready for each potential obstacle. As a result, he was able to keep his armies moving long enough to bypass an enemy's strong point and attack at an unsuspecting, weaker sector.

Most of us need to be reminded of the need for alternative plans. You may not be able to serve Christ in India this month. You may, however, be able to serve Him in your hometown. My grand design may need to give way to another. That other plan may appear to be less desirable, but it may actually contain the potential for greater accomplishment. Often, when stuck between the big thing we *cannot* do and the little thing we *will not* do, we end up doing nothing.

There is more to every moment than meets the eye. The delay at the airport may lead us to a person interested in Christ and salvation, and a frustration is turned into a golden opportunity. In each of our thwarted plans we can be sure that a sovereign God has a purpose. I will never forget the time that a last minute change in plans caused me to travel to London a day earlier than I expected. The flight I originally intended to be on crashed into a field in the Illinois countryside, and all perished. To second-guess the God who presides above our lives is to make a great mistake.

Impatience may well be evidence of stupidity. To fret in the midst of a traffic jam or cry over spilled milk is a waste of time. When nothing can be done about a circumstance, only fools rage, snarl, and pound the walls. The wise will see delay as opportunity. Many a noble thought, great idea, or availing prayer has come from seemingly lost moments. The wise will learn not to waste them.

Impatience also comes when we believe that we haven't got something we deserve or that others have been served first, paid more, or received a disproportionate amount of the credit. Impatient at such unfairness, we may rage and demand our rights. But we have no rights. You and I deserve nothing whatsoever in life except death and hell. Anything better is more than we deserve. It is not justice that we need but mercy.

Patience is the process of fitting properly into God's plans. Without patience, I will never fit into that plan and will never see the design of God fulfilled in my life.

I must give a word of warning here. God is determined to produce patience in our lives, and He will use various means to bring that about. That may well include a process called tribulation. As a part of His design, He may allow our problems to multiply until we are overwhelmed. Then we have no choice but to stand still and await the salvation of the Lord. "Having done all, to stand" (Ephesians 6:13) is the final keystone in the arch of patience. The Lord calls Himself "the God of patience" (Romans 15:5) and calls us to exercise patience. That patience will produce the persistence whereby we can run the race set before us until the end of time.

If we find ourselves resisting this divine process, we would do well to heed the question asked by the Lord Himself, "Hast thou considered my servant Job?" (Job 1:8). More than ever, in these impatient times, we should consider Job.

This godly patriarch suffered the loss of everything, including family, friends, wealth, possessions, and physical health. Despite the suggestion of his wife that he should curse God and die, he refused to doubt the Lord but continued patiently to wait on Him. Despite the humanistic advice of his philosopher friends, Job's patience did not fail. In his testimony Job gives us some of the greatest statements of faith found in the Bible, producing a testimony that stands for all time. Job had no expectations for a quick solution to his problems. He made no such demands upon God. He knew nothing of the miracle deliverance by some faith-formula. He knew that he could only rest his case with God and wait patiently for an answer, conceding in advance the wisdom and rightness of anything that God would do.

Job did not know whether he would live or die. He knew only that God presided over his life and had not forgotten him. In all of his tribulations, Job did not sin by renouncing God or cursing Him with his lips. He left us with a statement demonstrating the result of patience: "For I know that my redeemer liveth, and that he shall stand at the latter day upon the earth: and though after my skin worms destroy this body, yet in my flesh shall I see God" (Job 19:25-26).

The New Testament calls us to this kind of patience. The call comes in many ways; the lesson of Job is only one of them. The patience produced during trials keeps us thinking straight, walking in faith, and avoiding the foolishness of our times. May we let patience have her perfect work.

What "perfect work" is produced as we abide under pressures, problems, difficulties, and circumstances we cannot change? Many a tired believer may insist, "There are no real rewards. I keep on persisting, but the path appears to be endless." There are those who would like to kick over the traces and escape the burdens that press upon them. We cannot deny that there are burdens in life. Each of us faces something different: the birth of a retarded child, the approach of financial failure, the cruelty of an unloving spouse, the criticism of an ungrateful boss.

Some roads seem never to end or give way to an easier path. The much-touted solutions that apparently work for others do not work for us. When do we quit?

When do we turn in our resignation to God and an-
nounce that we are no longer willing to live the Christian
life? When do we throw in the towel and look for something less demanding?

The answer is never. Why? Because our circumstances are appointed by God, and any other circumstances will take us out of His will and into deeper
troubles than those we are in. Many a foolish husband or
wife believes the grass is greener on the other side of the
fence, only to get there and find a desert. They may wish
a thousand times that they had not tried to direct their
own course.

We find a remarkable promise in 2 Timothy 2:12:
"If we suffer, we shall also reign with him." This is
God's promise to those who live faithfully for Him. We
must note that the word *suffer* here is nearly the same as
the one Peter uses for *patience*. The word Peter used
means "an abiding under." This word is from the same
root and means "to remain under." It means "sustained"
—despite circumstances. We are told that the exercise of
patience—called "suffering" in this passage—produces
the result that "we shall also reign with him." That is
one of the most remarkable promises in the New Testament. It means that the need for patience will one day
end and be succeeded by the greatest rewards imagina-
ble. If we do not run away from the problems of life, we
will eventually be moved from those problems to a position of leadership in the eternal kingdom.

What problem in life poses a burden so great that it
is not overcome by the anticipated joy of reigning with
Christ? What pain, what suffering, what indignation
holds any weight when put next to an eternity of serving
in the rulership of the universe? The answer is that nothing whatsoever can compare! That is almost exactly the
declaration of Paul when he said, "For I reckon that the

sufferings of this present time are not worthy to be compared with the glory which shall be revealed in us" (Romans 8:18).

One winter's day, I was thinking of this while watching the snow fall. Here are my impressions of that moment:

Winter

How cold the snow must be
And yet the earth it warms
Protecting now the seeds of spring
'Gainst later, colder storms.

How hard our trials seem
When in the grip of pain
But God, in grace, allows them all
For future, greater gain.

Let minds then be renewed
Let hearts with courage sing
For seeds, by winter's trials fed
Will blossom into spring.

The summer's harvest comes
Whose bounty bids us learn
That faith amid the snows will bring
An hundred-fold return.

Patience is a faith-investment in the glory to come.

Godliness

7

The Imperative of Godliness

B efore that unfortunate afternoon in the Garden of Eden, life was wonderful for the two people who made up the entire population of the earth. Adam and Eve enjoyed every good thing in abundance. Being made in the image of God, they were intelligent, strong, and thoroughly capable of subduing the earth as God had commanded them.

Had Adam and Eve retained their original state, they never would have died. But Eve and then Adam yielded to the serpent's temptation, and death came into the world. Before that moment, they were in a beautiful, pristine state. They existed on a level far above the present condition of the human race. It is difficult to imagine what man was like then by viewing him as he is now. It would require something like trying to reconstruct the original version of an aircraft from its wreckage. If we knew nothing of flying, we would hardly suspect that it had once soared above the earth. The material would be the same; the capability of flight, however, would be lost.

The Fall of man had a similar devastating effect. We have today only shattered images of the beings we were before the Fall. And as it is with man, so it is with society. Today's world is filled with violence, turmoil, and degeneration—evidence of man's fallen condition. For a glimpse into the evil nature of mankind, we need only read the daily newspaper. As in the days of Noah, our world is full of people whose every imagination of the heart is only evil continually.

But is the darkness unbroken? Are there no circles of light in the otherwise black landscape? Happily, the answer to these questions is encouraging. In this world of evil, there are still glimmers, gleams, and sometimes beacons of marvelous light. Despite the darkness they shine, furnishing illumination and direction to many.

What are these lights in the world? They are Christians—Christians who have started with faith and added virtue, knowledge, and self-control. They are those who patiently labor as imitators of the King, who rules the kingdom of light. They are those who now add to their spiritual credentials the imperative of godliness.

What is godliness? It is "perfecting holiness in the fear of God." It is the call to be like God. It is to endeavor to resemble Him in speech, demeanor, appearance, conduct—all things. The word in Scripture is *eusebeia*, which means "to be devout." It is a call to a life characterized by a godward attitude, a life that seeks to please Him.

The pursuit of godliness has been outlined for us by David, a man after God's own heart, in his classic comparison of the godly and the ungodly. To understand the basis of the godly life, we need look no further than these six verses.

Blessed is the man that walketh not in the counsel of
the ungodly, nor standeth in the way of sinners, nor
sitteth in the seat of the scornful. But his delight is in
the law of the Lord, and in his law doth he meditate
day and night. And he shall be like a tree planted by
the rivers of water, that bringeth forth his fruit in his
season; his leaf also shall not wither; and whatsoever
he doeth shall prosper. The ungodly are not so: but are
like the chaff which the wind driveth away. Therefore
the ungodly shall not stand in the judgment, nor sinners in the congregation of the righteous. For the Lord
knoweth the way of the righteous: but the way of the
ungodly shall perish. (Psalm 1)

There are two kinds of people in the world—the
godly and the ungodly. Each of us must aspire to the righteous, godly side of the ledger. Everyone who aspires to
godliness must ask, "What must I do to be godly?" Notice
the teaching of Scripture.

The godly man does not consort or counsel with
sinners. A weak Christian will deface his testimony and
ruin his reputation and spiritual effectiveness by imitat-
ing the wrong crowd and sitting in the seat of the scornful. By listening to the counsel of the ungodly he becomes a cynic rather than a pursuer of God's will.

The godly person is one who delights in and medi-
tates on the Word of God. He makes it a day and night
occupation. As his heart is quickened and his mind renewed by the washing of the Word, he becomes more like
God.

The godly person brings forth fruit, and his activities prosper. An old song says that some will have "nothing but leaves for the Master." Their foliage is evident,
but fruit is conspicuously absent in their lives. The works
of the ungodly will not stand on Judgment Day, and they

will perish. Everything the sinner gains he will lose—his possessions, reputation, and then life itself will be gone.

The call to godliness is the call to the only kind of success that matters. There is something worse than failure in this world. What is that? It is to succeed at something that doesn't matter. That characterizes the work of every person whose life is not committed to the will of Jesus Christ.

Consider the millions of the citizens of the city of man grinding their days away in futility. Even those who think of themselves as purposeful are accomplishing things of no lasting value. Most of the people on earth travel around in little circles going nowhere. When they die their lives will show no eternal consequence.

How different are the accomplishments of those committed to the eternal purposes of God. To live a godly life is not easy, but it is abundantly possible.

We can rejoice that in the pursuit of godliness, as with all things, we will have help from the Lord. God intends that every Christian become more like Jesus Christ. We are predestinated to be conformed to the image of His Son (Romans 8:29). Having believed the gospel, the Christian comes under the fashioning of the Lord Himself. God will use every circumstance, every association, every experience of life to bring His children to the point that they reflect His holiness. To resist this working of God is to bring ourselves to defeat. To cooperate with this working of God is the highest form of spiritual wisdom. Seeking first the kingdom of God and His righteousness is the wisest course we can take.

How can we cooperate with God to produce godliness in our lives? Certainly, the first step is to concentrate on God. There's a principle that says we tend to become like the object of our affection. We imitate the people we admire. We attempt to talk like them, walk like them, and resemble them. We wisely, then, are advised in the Bible to make Jesus Christ the object of our contemplation.

The writer of Hebrews tells us that we are involved in a great race that reaches through time into eternity. To win such a race, we will need strength and motivation. Where will we get these qualities? The scriptural answer is "looking unto Jesus the author and finisher of our faith; who for the joy that was set before him endured the cross, despising the shame, and is set down at the right hand of the throne of God" (Hebrews 12:2).

So when our energy begins to fail in the pursuit of godliness, we are to look to our supreme example, Jesus Christ.

The writer then says, "For consider him that endured such contradiction of sinners against himself, lest ye be wearied and faint in your minds. Ye have not yet resisted unto blood, striving against sin" (Hebrews 12:3-4). To those who would tire in battle come the stinging words, "Ye have not yet resisted unto blood." We have no right to complain, and it is too soon to quit anywhere short of death in the battle for righteousness.

An even stronger call to conform ourselves to Christ is given in the command "Let this mind be in you, which was also in Christ Jesus" (Philippians 2:5). The mind of Christ is the gift given to every Christian and the call of conformity to that mind is extended to each of us. We should think each day about the program God has for us.

In every circumstance of life, one should ask, "What is God's plan in this?" "What is the spiritual principle behind this event?" "What new spiritual quality does God intend to develop in me through this circumstance?" No event in life is without spiritual value to the person pursuing godliness.

One should then ask, "What would God have me do?"

A generation ago Charles Sheldon wrote a book entitled *In His Steps.* In this classic Christian work, Sheldon has each of his characters, when faced with a dilemma, ask, "What would Jesus do?" In the course of the book they face various questions of disharmony, dishonesty, and even disgrace. Their courses of action in light of their commitment to do what Jesus would do provides a fascinating outcome.

To do the will of God by the light that we have is the path to godliness. That lesson could be applied to each of our lives. Scripture teaches that Jesus Christ left us an example so that we could follow in His steps (John 13:15; 1 Peter 2:21). The Scriptures also tell us that we have the example of the prophets, the apostles, the angels, and, of course, the godly, consecrated, heroic believers whose lives are presented in the Word of God. In addition, we have the example of those who throughout the history of the church have ministered with distinction in their service to God. John Wesley expressed this aspiration when he wrote:

> To serve my present age
> My calling to fulfill;
> Oh may it all my powers engage
> To do my Master's will.

The believer who pursues this course of action will become a trusted illustration of truth—an example. His godly life will be used of the Lord to point the way to another who labors behind him. Each of us is an example —positive or negative—to someone. How tragic that the life of any believer should become an illustration of spiritual failure. How beautiful when we can offer a godly example. To fulfill that purpose is to be a light-bearer, projecting the image of Christ to a dark world. God's supreme instrument in accomplishing His will in the world is the life and testimony of the godly Christian.

Knowing something of this dark and unfriendly world, we find a related question coming to mind. "Why doesn't God intervene in history in a more direct and powerful way?" "Why doesn't He give us something more reliable than the fragile lives of believing Christians?" "Why does He appear to leave so much responsibility to us and our own devices?" There are times when we would like to cry out, "God, where are You?" Where is God when the darkness threatens to smother us? Where is God, who could so easily deliver us?

Some believe that these questions themselves are evidence of insufferable faithlessness. "God is right here," they say. "He is at your beck and call." They tell us to claim the promises and command His response, then we will instantly and abundantly have whatever we need. They promote a doctrine of miracles upon request. The wand of prayer is lifted and—presto—no problems! God always intervenes, instantly fulfilling all desires. There is no need for patient, godly, sacrificial living. Suffering is evidence of insufficient faith.

This doctrine is, of course, false. It should be rejected by all who have read the Word or even lived a bit of life. Anyone who has lost a child in an accident, seen a beloved wife endure cancer, failed to prevent a son's divorce, or watched a loved one die will reject the false teaching that promises God's intervention in all situations.

If not by His personal intervention, how then does God work in the world? Let us not forget the personal intervention of Jesus Christ into history. Anyone who would argue that God has not done enough should take another look at Christ's death on Calvary. In this one event the love of God was demonstrated irrefutably and forever. The argument that God does not care is forever proved false. The death, burial, and resurrection of Christ is the evidence on which God rests His case. He is the loving Intervenor in human history.

In dying for us Christ worked the great *external* work. He died in space and time, in flesh and blood, for all the world to see and believe. He arose and declared Himself alive "by many infallible proofs" and before many witnesses. This is the message He has sent to the world.

How then does He plan to give that message? He does it by calling godly witnesses—not magicians. A magician is one who creates illusions. Spiritual magicians pervert the gospel with their fanciful illusions. Seldom in Christian history have so many foolishly paid so much for so little.

The Lord's program is different. He calls witnesses whose testimony is verified by godliness. These witnesses know the blessing of sins forgiven; they have believed in the Christ of Calvary. We must recognize that God, having spoken through His Son and His written Word, is now silent as to new, verbal revelation. He has called others to speak for Him and has appointed them His ambassadors in this world. How do we know these witnesses to be true? The testimony is their godliness. They are "like God." They become "living Bibles" for the world to read.

Anyone who believes that godliness is not essential to Christian living should take another look at the increasingly godless society in which we live. One of the strongest descriptions of the world in which we live is given in conjunction with the coming of Jesus Christ in judgment. Jude says, "Behold, the Lord cometh with ten thousands of his saints, to execute judgment upon all, and to convince all that are ungodly among them of all their ungodly deeds which they have ungodly committed, and of all their hard speeches that ungodly sinners have spoken against him" (vv. 14b-15). The word *ungodly* is used four times in that single verse of Scripture.

Can anyone doubt that this is the way God sees this world? Can anyone doubt that the godly life, lived in the midst of such ungodliness, will be set apart? Godliness is imperative to service for Christ. As we move toward the end of the age, this imperative may become the single most important credential of those taking the message of Christ to a darkening world.

Finally, who are these witnesses? They are you and I. "You are my witnesses," said our Lord Jesus. This He said to His disciples and to each one of us. What credentials do we have? We are to have godliness! We are to be as much like God—like our Lord Jesus—as we can possibly be.

The godliness Peter advocates is established only through steadfastness. The steadfast Christian will stay true to God, establish himself on the path to godliness, and be characterized by love.

There was a time when I sought to discover the qualities essential to godly living and to learn what I must do to achieve them. It soon became clear to me that these qualities are developed slowly and progressively. They do not appear suddenly but are acquired as we attempt to perform the will of God. Neither godliness nor any of the other virtues is achieved in an instant. They do not come about as a result of one traumatic experience. There is no breakthrough that takes us suddenly from a low to a high quality of living.

Yet Peter tells us, "Add to your faith . . . godliness" —and we know that it can be done. This is to be our great credential. Without this credential our words are empty. One may claim spiritual gifts, work miracles, and speak with great eloquence, but these and a thousand other claims are nothing without godliness. We must respond to this call. It promises great gain, both in this world and in the world to come.

Brotherly Kindness

8

The Imperative of Brotherly Kindness

Every newborn child is a unique individual. He will grow to become a distinct person, and, as he grows, his uniqueness will become more apparent. To have any understanding of the nature of people we must remember that, first of all, each one is an individual.

Each child also takes on a unique set of relationships. He is, first, a member of a family. As his world grows, his relationships will become more varied and meaningful. In fact, a growing realization of the importance of relationships is a mark of maturity. No man lives unto himself, and no man dies unto himself. If not for the union of two separate personalities—his mother and his father—the child would have no existence at all. If not for healthy relationships in his life, his happiness—and even his survival—would be impossible.

One of our goals in life is to foster and develop relationships with others. Each of us has a family of some sort—a mother, father, sister, brother, spouse, or child. Each of us has—or should have—friendships in various stages of development. The person who is happiest is the one with the ability to make the relationships of life happy ones. The wise person determines to get along with those people with whom he must live, work, or interact. One who takes no time to build relationships is soon isolated and unhappy. He is also foolish, ignoring the fact that relationships with people are one of the most important aspects of our lives on earth.

That is true for everyone. However, it is crucial for the Christian. He is a member of the most important family in the universe: the family of God. He must not ignore that relationship, for to do so will leave him a weak, unproductive Christian. What is the ingredient that makes relationships fulfilling? In Scripture it is called "brotherly kindness." So it is that Peter calls us to add brotherly kindness to our list of imperatives.

In Scripture this is the familiar word *philadelphia*. It literally means "to have tender affection toward your brother." It means to cherish, to highly regard, to think well of fellow believers.

We should note that this call to brotherly kindness comes after the call to godliness. Is it possible that the Lord is reminding us that some within the Body of Christ may be long on godliness but short on brotherly kindness? To concentrate on spirituality is commendable, but to forget to be kind to others in the process is unforgivable.

We may recognize this imbalance in those around us. Sister Smith takes on a look of transcendence when the hymns are sung but has only harsh words for her energetic children at the end of the service. Brother Jones is quick with a word of testimony in prayer meeting but has only complaints for the customers at his grocery business the rest of the week. Deacon McGafferty smiles at everyone as he shakes hands at the church door on Sunday morning, but we soon learn that his real goal is to sell us something the next time he sees us.

We have each met those believers (sometimes even in places of leadership) who had commendable spiritual qualities but who were lacking in brotherly kindness. More important, though, we need to recognize this tendency in ourselves. We are called to develop genuine kindness as we relate to others.

Not so long ago, most of us lived in a world characterized by what the Bible calls "natural affection." In the days when Christian thinking was reflected in much of the Western world, we took for granted a commodity called "common grace." Grace existed in the church to the extent that it spilled over and bubbled out into the world. In those days of common grace, people tended to be honest, generous, and helpful to others. No more than a generation ago, one could reasonably expect help if he had an overheated car, a flat tire, or needed change for a telephone call. People generally believed one another and expressed a willingness to help one another. Common grace produced a certain civility that made it possible for communities to maintain reasonable expectations of safety.

In our present world, this remarkable quality seems to be disappearing. The woman whose automobile stalls by the roadside cannot be confident that the man who stops to help does not have assault or even murder on his mind. In few cities does the occupant of a home dare to open a front door to the ring of a bell. He suspects— sometimes correctly—that the one who waits at the front door may pose a danger to his life.

Around the world we find the same hostilities and fears. The airplane that carries us from Rome to Athens may be the object of a terrorist bombing. The airport, the bank, the shopping center, or the public street could in an instant be shaken with the clatter of machine-gun fire as the terrorist performs his deadly ideological duty.

And on another level, the same attitudes exist. In the conduct of business, materialism or the exploitation of ruthless advantage becomes the order of the day. Presumption and exploitation at every level—government, financial life, religious life, education, and neighborhood —appear to be the order of the day.

The fact of man's inhumanity is well known. That inhumanity appears to be growing stronger in our time. And the Word of God has warned us of the peril that will come upon society as we move toward the end of the age. It promises that "evil men and seducers shall [become] worse and worse, deceiving, and being deceived" (2 Timothy 3:13).

Scripture clearly announces that one of the reasons the judgment of God comes upon the children of men is that they allow themselves to become "without natural affection" (Romans 1:31). No longer influenced by the smallest measure of common grace, the world becomes an unkind, hateful place in which to live. Who can doubt that this tide is moving in our time?

What an opportunity for the church to provide a contrast. What a difference the lives of Christians should be to the emotional, moral tenor of our world. In such times, the call to brotherly kindness becomes even more important. We who believe the gospel must take the first steps to re-introduce kindness in these times. But how?

First of all, we must remember that we belong to one another. The Bible clearly teaches that we are members of one body. That means I am necessary to you and you are necessary to me. I belong to you, and you belong to me. We are members of "the church, which is his body, the fulness of him that filleth all in all" (Ephesians

1:22-23). We are admonished to "walk worthy of the vo-
cation wherewith ye are called, with all lowliness and
meekness, with longsuffering, forbearing one another in
love; endeavoring to keep the unity of the Spirit in the
bond of peace" (4:1-3). We are together to work "for the
edifying of the body of Christ: till we all come in the unity of the faith, and of the knowledge of the Son of God,
unto a perfect man, unto the measure of the stature of the
fullness of Christ" (vv. 12-13). We are called upon to
"grow up into him in all things, which is the head, even
Christ: from whom the whole body fitly joined together
and corr   .ted by that which every joint supplieth, according to the effectual working and the measure of every
part, maketh increase of the body unto the edifying of itself in love" (vv. 15-16). No Christian should ever be
without a sense of belonging. We belong to one another.

We should seek to express that sense of belonging.
Scripture admonishes, "Let us consider one another to
provoke unto love and to good works: not forsaking the
assembling of ourselves together, as the manner of some
is; but exhorting one another: and so much the more, as
ye see the day approaching" (Hebrews 10:24-25).

In assembling ourselves together, we find a mutual
participation in the things of the Lord that is impossible
in isolation. When Christians worship the Lord together,
sing the songs of the faith together, give the offering together, listen to the preaching together, and say "amen"
together they build a unity that lasts after the service is
over.

I'm encouraged to see a recent tendency in church
architecture calculated to foster interaction. In most old-
er churches, the worshiper who reaches the back of the
church finds himself out in the street and on the way
home. Now, as church auditoriums grow, so also do the
lobbies. These provide an atmosphere for greetings, con-

versations, comments on the service, the meeting of new people, and other interactions. The church that fosters the acquaintance and affection of Christians for one another is building something lasting. Indeed, this affection—when genuine—will continue to grow as Christians continue to love and cherish one another.

In my travels I have had the opportunity to preach in churches across the world, and I've seen all types. There is the church that at the end of the benediction is instantly empty. Within five minutes the congregation has scattered to the four winds with hardly a lingering smile or handshake for one another. One cannot help but conclude that these Christians do not care for one another.

The contrasting church is wonderful to see. It is beautiful to be in a service where the benediction is merely the beginning of the fellowship time. Clusters of people—young and old—join in animated, radiant conversation. These occasions of fellowship extend on to the local coffee shop or someone's home. It seems that these Christians genuinely appreciate one another and find it difficult to say good-bye. This is one of the genuine blessings this side of heaven. It is called Christian fellowship.

The fellowship of the saints is commended by Peter. He calls us to make it the diligent pursuit of our lives. To be obedient to this call, we should not forsake the assembling of ourselves together. We should diligently work to find ways to help one another. That is exactly what Scripture teaches in saying, "As we have therefore opportunity, let us do good unto all men, especially unto them who are of the household of faith" (Galatians 6:10). As opportunity presents itself, we are to do good to all people, but *especially* to fellow believers.

Christians have a special relationship with one another. We are to have an inside track to call upon the help of another. We are to be especially forward in extending that help to another believer in Christ.

We are to highly esteem one another. We are to be the last to believe the worst about one another. The time may be approaching when Christians will need to draw up the wagons and set up a common defense against the assaults of a hostile world. Shoulder to shoulder, we may have to stand against the encroaching darkness. That will call for a special relationship.

We are to assemble even more so "as ye see the day approaching." What day? Certainly, this day to which the Scriptures refer is the day of deterioration in our troubled world. It is the day of the Great Tribulation; the day of the rise of the Antichrist; the day of the final judgment of God. Ultimately, we are reminded of the day when we shall stand before Christ and give an answer for our lives. This will include not only our individual accomplishments but an account of how we have worked together to accomplish the will of Christ.

Let us also remember that one aspect of brotherly kindness is to refrain from the opposite—brotherly animosity. Regarding this, Paul told us, "For, brethren, ye have been called unto liberty; only use not liberty for an occasion to the flesh, but by love serve one another. For all the law is fulfilled in one word, even in this; thou shalt love thy neighbor as thyself. But if ye bite and devour one another, take heed that ye be not consumed one of another" (Galatians 5:13-15).

Could Christians be involved in biting and devouring one another? God forbid! How will we ever muster the strength to oppose the work of the world or assault the ramparts of the devil if there is dissent in our ranks?

We note that it is not uncommon for Christians to disagree. Within the legitimate province of Christianity, there are Calvinists and Arminians; pietists and activists; and scores of denominations, churches, and individuals —all with deeply held convictions. Such differences are not bad. In fact, if characterized by self-control, discussions of our differences could be marvelously instructive and enlightening. Intelligent Christian debate would be certainly be more profitable than the mindless assent that characterizes many assemblies today.

The call to brotherly kindness, however, forbids us from doing damage to one another. If we allow dissent to carry us to that point, we are warned of the possibility of being consumed by one another. In the name of brotherly kindness, then, how shall we handle Christian differences?

To begin with, we must be sure that the person with whom we disagree is, in fact, a Christian. We are not called upon to find common agreement with the world. We are not here to conduct a forum with the enemies of the gospel in order to find a basis of agreement. We need to learn to tell the difference between a fellow belligerent in some human cause and a brother in Christ. Having decided this on the basis of sound doctrine, we must purpose to never let a discussion get out of hand.

I am frequently involved in debates at evangelical conventions, peace conferences, colleges, and the like. At such times, I have occasionally had the opportunity to become friends with the person whom I oppose. After one such debate, I had the opportunity to eat dinner with my opposition—an evangelical scholar of decidedly leftist persuasion. We had an animated—but friendly—discussion. We reminded ourselves that we each had a wife, children, spiritual opportunity, and many related, similar involvements. Because of that dinner, I understand this Christian leader somewhat better. We have even ex-

changed cordial correspondence since. Despite our differences, we were able to exercise brotherly kindness.

Over the years of public ministry I have received
many letters that express less than complete agreement
with the positions I have taken on radio, television, or in
print. I appreciate these because they are generally
thoughtful and intelligent. I value the suggestions made,
and occasionally—though not often—my opinion has been
changed.

There is also a practical way to build a relationship
with someone with whom we otherwise disagree. It is to
perform an act of kindness for that person entirely apart
from our spiritual views. I carry a pair of jumper cables in
the trunk of my automobile with exactly that purpose in
mind. It is my hope that I may have the opportunity to
give a jump-start to (or to receive one from) some believer
whose theology I may dislike. Even a pair of jumper cables becomes a bridge to friendship. We are responsible
to maintain a unity of spirit and a bond of peace with
fellow believers.

Whenever possible, loving-kindness should also
characterize our relationship with the world. Millions of
people in today's world know only hatred, vindictive-
ness, mistrust, and disappointment. Some have never
known kindness. The kindness of a Christian can be the
key that allows us to touch, indeed to win, the sin-dark-
ened life. We do well to wake up every morning and ask,
"What act of kindness could I bring this day to a person
who needs me?" That act of kindness could open the
door to spiritual opportunity. As the world becomes a
more hateful place each day, the kindness of a Christian
will stand out more brilliantly. We live in a time when
the practice of this imperative may bear more fruit than
ever, for time and for eternity.

How many foolish divisions within the church might never have happened if enough people practiced kindness toward one another? How many disagreements would be avoided by the presence of even a dash of brotherly kindness? How many destroyed reputations would be preserved but for the unkindness of a gossip or a scandalmonger? How many broken marriages would be intact if kindly affection replaced hate, insults, and maliciousness?

Remember, we must be not only godly but also kind. We must stand straight as soldiers of the faith, but we must bend deeply to offer a cup of kindness to those in need. Roland Sill said in "The Fools' Prayer":

> The ill-time truth we might have kept
> Who knows how sharp it pierced and stung?
> The word we had not sense to say
> Who knows how gladly it had rung?
>
> These clumsy feet still in the mire
> Go crushing blossoms without end
> These hard, well-meaning hands we thrust
> Among the heartstrings of a friend.

How different the world would be with a dash of kindness. How transformed the church would be if brotherly kindness was a major ingredient in every conversation. May that wonderful store of common grace once again fill the church and spill out to the world. May it yet come to pass because we have heeded the call to pursue brotherly kindness.

And what are the results of brotherly kindness? Scripture tells us that they are characterized by abundant return. We read, "Give, and it shall be given unto you; good measure, pressed down, and shaken together, and running over, shall men give into your bosom. For with the same measure that ye [measure] it shall be measured to you again" (Luke 6:38). Surely this is speaking of more than just giving money.

The performance of acts of kindness and generosity brings the potential of multiplied return. Acts of brotherly kindness tap into a hidden wellspring in the hearts of others and stimulate them to respond in similar fashion. Kindness has a marvelous way of propagating itself. The hearts of the unregenerate are often won through acts of kindness. What wonderful things we could accomplish for the Lord if brotherly kindness flowed from the heart of every believer.

We have the testimony of history to show the fruit borne as a result of kindness. We find a classic example in the story of the servant of Abraham sent to find Isaac a wife. When he reached Abraham's homeland, he prayed:

> Oh Lord God of my master Abraham, I pray thee, send me good speed this day, and shew kindness unto my master Abraham. Behold, I stand here by the well of water; and the daughters of the men of the city come out to draw water: and let it come to pass, that the damsel to whom I shall say, Let down thy pitcher, I pray thee, that I may drink; and she shall say, Drink, and I will give thy camels drink also: let the same be she that thou hast appointed for thy servant Isaac; and thereby shall I know that thou hast shewed kindness unto my master. (Genesis 24:12-14)

The servant prayed that the wife of Isaac would be revealed to him by an act of kindness. That prayer was soon answered.

> And it came to pass, before he had done speaking, that, behold, Rebekah came out, who was born to Bethuel,

son of Milcah, the wife of Nahor, Abraham's brother, with her pitcher upon her shoulder. And the damsel was very fair to look upon, a virgin, neither had any man known her: and she went down to the well, and filled her pitcher, and came up. And the servant ran to meet her, and said, Let me, I pray thee, drink a little water of thy pitcher. And she said, Drink, my lord: and she hastened, and let down her pitcher upon her hand, and gave him drink. And when she had done giving him drink, she said, I will draw water for thy camels also, until they have done drinking. (vv. 15-19)

When Rebekah had fulfilled her act of kindness, the servant honored her and entreated her help. "The man took a golden earring of half a shekel weight, and two bracelets for her hands of ten shekels weight of gold; and said, Whose daughter art thou? Tell me, I pray thee: is there room in thy father's house for us to lodge in?" (vv. 22-23).

The results of this story are well known. Rebekah became the chosen wife of Isaac and one of the mothers of Israel. Her act of kindness was reciprocated in that she became part of the line of redemption. Giving a drink of water in the name of the Lord may not seem like much; however, such acts of kindness have been used to alter the course of history.

In the book of Ruth we have a similar story. In obedience to faith and the leading of God, Ruth acted in kindness toward Boaz, her kinsman. He responded by saying, "Blessed be thou of the Lord, my daughter: for thou hast shewed more kindness in the latter end than at the beginning, inasmuch as thou followedst not young men, whether poor or rich. And now, my daughter, fear not; I will do to thee all that thou requirest: for all the city of my people doth know that thou art a virtuous woman" (Ruth 3:10-11).

The result of Ruth's kindness is beautifully record-ed. She became the wife of Boaz and part of the lineage of the Messiah.

The illustration is clear. Kindness has a way of mul-tiplying itself. And God promises that kindness will bring abundant return—if not in this life, certainly in the one to come.

If this simple quality were to flow from the lives of believers, who can imagine the multiplying effect upon our society? It wouldn't require anything profound or fancy or even too theological—just simple brotherly kindness. With this gentle blessing flowing through the church to the world, who can doubt that everything would be different?

Love

9

The Imperative of Love

S
ometimes I think Christians could profit from a trip into the past. We would do well to detach ourselves for a moment and travel back through history, moving with wonder and anticipation through the years. As we went, we would need to shed our pretensions, our prejudices, our presumed accomplishments, and our self-appreciation.

We would travel back through nearly two thousand years to a rocky hillside outside the city of Jerusalem. There we would stand and savor the day when time stopped and started again with a new purpose—the day when the living Son of God was executed by man, thereby dying for the sins of the world.

What would it be like to observe Christ's pain as the nails were driven into His hands? Can we imagine watching as His feet were pierced? Can we conceive of that sacred head bearing a crown of thorns? Isaiah speaks of these things, saying, "His visage was so marred more than any man, and his form more than the sons of men" (Isaiah 52:14).

If we knew something of the life, the ministry, the compassion of Christ in the days preceding this one, we would be at a loss to explain this event. We would say it was impossible that anyone, especially Jesus Christ, could commit crimes meriting such a cruel execution.

For the beginning of an explanation, we would need to look again to the words of Isaiah: "He is despised and rejected of men; a man of sorrows, and acquainted with grief: and we hid as it were our faces from him; he was despised, and we esteemed him not. Surely he hath borne our griefs, and carried our sorrows: yet we did esteem him stricken, smitten of God, and afflicted" (Isaiah 53:3-4).

But still, we would ask, Why has this awful cataract of grief and sorrow come upon the holy, harmless Son of God? We should read on with astonishment and gratefulness. "But he was wounded for our transgressions, he was bruised for our iniquities: the chastisement of our peace was upon him; and with his stripes we are healed. All we like sheep have gone astray; we have turned every one to his own way; and the Lord hath laid on him the iniquity of us all" (vv. 5-6).

In this most significant event of all history, the Lord Jesus Christ suffered in our place, purchasing the righteousness that becomes ours if we believe in Him. On this day the Old Covenant was superseded by a New Covenant written in the blood of Christ. There began the covenant of divine grace, whereby all who come as sinners to the Savior are washed clean and made acceptable by His atoning work.

Volumes could not contain an adequate description of the scene that day. The Roman soldiers were there. Having nailed Him to the cross, they sat down and watched after casting lots for His garment. Not knowing who He was, they saw this as just another execution of an enemy of Rome. Then came the darkness! Then came the earthquake! They may have then asked, "Why?"

The rulers of the Jews were there. They were bringing to pass their own avowed statement, "We will not have this man to reign over us" (Luke 19:14). Little did they dream of the desolation that would come upon them by reason of this occasion. They should have asked, "Why?"

The multitudes were there. They looked on with a mixture of bewilderment, sadistic interest, and compassion. They could not fathom the issue in question. Few realized that eternal life and death were at stake in what was taking place. Did someone ask, "Why?"

Mary, His mother, was there. Her heart was pierced with sorrow at the sight of her Son dying in such agony. Surely, she knew by this time His true identity. Her son was her God! Her heart must have held a mixture of adoration, bewilderment, hope, and despair. She surely asked, "Why?"

Some of His disciples were there. Most of them were crushed, believing that that all was lost, that His promises and presence would be gone forever. Only later did their hearts burn within as He identified Himself to them on the Emmaus road. Then their grieving hearts asked, "Why?"

Barabbas was, doubtless, there. He had been released as a prisoner of the Jews. Now his place of execution was taken by this divine Substitute. We hope that Barabbas came to faith in the One who redeemed his body and offered to redeem his soul.

Satan was there. Having filled his servant Judas with the spirit of betrayal, he was now looking, perhaps gleefully, at the results of his plans. If he knew, he would not admit that this day—far from being his moment of victory—was the day of his judgment. He never understood why.

The Father was there. This was the one to whom Christ spoke, first with the question, "My God, my God, why hast thou forsaken me?" (Matthew 27:46; Mark 15:34). Then, three agonizing hours later, with the words, "Father, into thy hands I commend my spirit" (Luke 23:46). Of Him Christ asked, "Why?"

You and I were there. Our life, our death, our eternity, was on the block at Calvary. We recognize our presence there when we believe. With the apostle Paul we can say, "I am crucified with Christ" (Galatians 2:20).

Here we see the death of the Son of God at Calvary —costly beyond estimation. We must ask, "Why?"

Yes, in looking upon this event, we are left with the fundamental questions: Why? Why did He die? What made Him willing to give His life?

Complex answers could be devised, but a simple answer can be given in one word—*love*. It was the love of God, the love of Christ for a lost humanity that impelled Him to this awful and wonderful act of redemption. "In this was manifested the love of God toward us, because that God sent his only begotten Son into the world, that we might live through him. Herein is love, not that we loved God, but that he loved us, and sent his Son to be the propitiation for our sins" (1 John 4:9-10). That's why!

This love is expressed in Scripture by the Greek word *agapao*. It has been described as "the characteristic word of Christianity, and since the spirit of revelation has used it to express ideas previously unknown, inquiry into its use, whether in Greek literature or in the Septuagint, throws but little light upon its distinctive meaning in the New Testament." God has taken this sublime word and endowed it with a meaning unknown in any other language. It can only be described in terms closely tied to the Creator of the universe. *Agapao* means "the love of God."

It is used in the New Testament to describe the nature of God. Volumes could not reveal the meaning of the phrase "God is love" (1 John 4:8). So exalted is this word in describing the intrinsic nature of the Lord that we may expect to find little other proper illustration of its essential meaning. And so it is. Love is explained in the New Testament, not in terms of its essence, but in terms of its activity. In the last analysis, its essence may well be beyond description, but its activity is well presented.

Its ultimate activity is that it is the motivation for the sacrifice of the life of Christ on Calvary. Because of that sacrifice, God is able to make history's most moving announcement, "God so loved the world, that he gave his only begotten Son, that whosoever believeth in him should not perish, but have everlasting life" (John 3:16). This act and this announcement are presented in Scripture as the essence of love. "But God commendeth his love toward us, in that, while we were yet sinners, Christ died for us" (Romans 5:8). The love of God is beyond description. That infinite meaning, according to the Word, is illustrated in its best sense in the death of Christ on Calvary. How fathomless is the depth of that sacrifice and the depth of the love that allowed it.

Now it is your turn to express, to embody that love —yours and mine! That same quality of divine love is enjoined upon us. Peter uses the same word to name the crowning imperative of the Christian life. We are to add to our faith virtue, knowledge, self-control, patience, godliness, brotherly kindness, and now, *agapao* itself—the love of God. Such love is to characterize our lives. It is the final imperative. What a sublime, unbelievable call!

Is it possible? Are we to become the bearers of, the custodians of, the love of God in our world? Yes, indeed!

Each Christian is commanded and enabled to be a walking illustration of divine love in all that he says, thinks, and does. Christ is not here, but we are His representatives. As divine ambassadors we are human embodiments of the love of Christ. But remember, we must not be merely transported by the ambiguous glory of the loving commission placed upon us to reflect His love. We must be doers of His love!

Love, to be real, must take an object. What then must be the first object of the love grafted into our hearts, hearts that were once characterized by hatred, indifference, selfishness, and other opposites of the love of God.

The first object of our love must be the Lord Himself. The Christian faith is more than just a code of rules, a system of doctrine, or a set of practices. At its core, Christianity is a person. That person is God Himself, in three persons—the Father, Son, and Holy Spirit. God is the first object of our love.

This has been the mark of every mature Christian. In the early stages of the Christian life, we may have loved a thousand things. But, one by one, these things show themselves unworthy of affection. As we seek first the kingdom of God and His righteousness, these "things" —the incidentals of life—are added unto us. Maturity, then, brings our vision into proper focus—on the Lord Himself.

Paul, after many years of service, stated his fondest ambition. To the questions, What would you like to have most? What would it take to make you perfectly happy? Paul's answer was, "That I may know him, and the power of his resurrection, and the fellowship of his sufferings, being made conformable unto his death" (Philippians 3:10). Christ became the singular object of his deepest love. That love became the constraining force for everything he did.

As we mature, so it will be with us. As Christ becomes the object of our love, all other things fall into place. Because of that love, we are able to set right priorities. Because of that love, we do not grow tired in battle. Because of that love, we are able to discern between the good and the best and choose that which will glorify Christ.

Having settled on love for God, we are lead to a compelling love for the Body of Christ. The need for such love is presented to us in many ways, not the least of which is in the words "A new commandment I give unto you, That ye love one another; as I have loved you, that ye also love one another. By this shall all men know that you are my disciples, if ye have love one to another" (John 13:34-35). Love that wells up from the heart of the believer like a fountain, is also admonished to Him with the force of a commandment of our Lord.

In this matter of loving one another, we have the powerful help of the Holy Spirit. Indeed, the "fruit of the Spirit is love" (Galatians 5:22). Just as the life within the tree causes the fruit to appear, so the life within the believer—with the help of the Holy Spirit—produces beautiful fruit. But in our efforts to produce the fruit of the Spirit, we must remember an interesting fact. We cannot cause fruit to grow; but we are earnestly asked to cultivate it. We are to weed it, and prune it, and protect it; only God can produce it. So it is with the fruit of the Spirit in our lives.

The love of believers for one another becomes a great credential before the world. One of the primary reputations of the early church was established because Christians were known by their genuine love one for another. It is impossible to divide the ranks or lead astray a segment of the flock of believers who have between them that greatest of all magnetism, the attraction of love.

The church has been called to minister in a world without love. Today's society runs on greed, avarice, self-seeking, and ruthless advantage-taking. The life of the believer stands in contrast to this. Within the body of believers, the lonesome, the disenfranchised, and the lost can be accepted. The Christian life is distinguished by the promise that the love of God is shed upon our hearts by the Holy Spirit that is given unto us. The love of the brethren is the greatest concurrent advantage, next to sound doctrine, that the church has.

The object of our love, therefore, is also the world. The world is hateful, vindictive, degenerate, and lost. The world lives its life in the kind of darkness that makes its victims less lovely with every day that passes. Nevertheless these people are the objects of God's love and must be objects of our love. We were once members of that group. But while we were sinners, the love of God through other believers was extended to us. The ministry of extending the love of Christ to others now falls to us. Our ability to display that love is an increasing accurate marker of our Christian maturity.

In thinking on this emergent love of God, I wrote out of that moment's inspiration, the following lines:

Emergence

I see more clearly now,
The mists of morn have lifted
Revealing here the path of life
From which my heart had drifted.

For vision, indistinct in youth
Grows clearer with the years
If subject to the press of life
And washed by time and tears.

I love more purely now,
'Tis more than pure emotion
For feeling is to real love
As mountain stream to ocean.

And love invades the intellect
And love empowers the will
The heart endowing with a voice
That time can never still.

I move more surely now,
My life has found its reason
A holy purpose now pervades
Each day and every season.

For God has made me like Himself,
I see this now as never,
Perceiving this, I see in Him,
My destiny forever.

God calls us to embody this love in an unlovely world.

When we think of this call, however, we are faced with a problem. It is expressed in the questions: What is love? and, How should we develop it? The answer is not simple. The love of God is a quality that defies definition, just as God Himself is so high and holy as to be beyond definition.

We must not despair, however, because things that are difficult to understand, even if not definable in their *essence*, can often be defined by their *operation*. We may not be able to understand what they *are*, but we can understand what they *do*. That is true of such mysterious entities as light, electricity, thought, and many other things beyond our understanding. We know their effects, if not their essence. This can be applied to love as well.

The Lord has given us a description of love entirely in terms of what it does. We find it in 1 Corinthians 13.

This account tells us many things. First, we are told that if we speak with the tongues of men and angels, but without the love of God we do no more than make noise (v. 1). Apart from love, eloquence holds no significance.

Next, we are told that spiritual gifts are worth nothing without love (v. 2). These may include the gift of prophecy, the gift of miraculous understanding, the possession of all knowledge and all faith, even to the extent of removing mountains. But apart from the love of God, the person with such gifts has nothing.

Generosity apart from divine love is worthless (v. 3). One may bestow all of his goods to feed the poor and still accomplish nothing. One may even give his body to be burned and do so totally without profit. By this many will be reminded of the Buddhist priests on the streets of Vietnam during that war who covered themselves with gasoline and set themselves aflame. What did that accomplish? Nothing! Nothing whatsoever is significant unless it is accompanied by the love of God.

What, then, does love do? It suffers long and is kind. It does not envy or promote itself (v. 4). It is correct in its behavior, is not selfish or easily provoked, and does not think evil (v. 5).

It does not rejoice in iniquity but in truth (v. 6). It is eternally patient, bearing all things. It is full of faith, hope, and endurance (v. 7). Though many other things can and will fail, love does not (v. 8).

The love of God in our lives is the capstone of the imperatives. Love interacts completely with the other qualities and becomes the source of each of them. It is greater than faith, greater than hope; it is the greatest of all human endeavors.

Love must pervade the lives of all who believe the gospel in these last days. Christ warns us of a time when love will be put at risk because of sinful society: "Because iniquity shall abound, the love of many shall [grow] cold" (Matthew 24:12). The believer who possesses divine love will stand out from the crowd. He will shine in a dark world. We must pray to be delivered from the cynicism overtaking us in these days of iniquity. As sin continues to rise, the love of God must continue to rise in our lives.

10

Moving On Up

Preparing for the life to come is one of the chief purposes of our time here on earth. Even while we are here, our true citizenship is not in any nation but in heaven. We anticipate the moment when we shall move to that world, stepping from the shadows of time into the substance of eternity. We are to have no permanent dwelling place in this world but are to be seekers of an eternal city whose builder and maker is God.

Many find these ideas preposterous. They believe that talk of a better, future life is at best irresponsible, and at worst a destructive lie. To suggest that a future life will hold meaning and purpose may elicit their tolerant smiles. To insist that the life to come will be glorious, eternal, and more "real" than this one is to risk one's reputation.

It is not the Christian, however, but society that is irrational. Having given themselves over to a thousand errors that seem sensible by present standards, the men and women of our time have ceased to love truth. Believing that this life is everything, the people of our age have embraced what the Bible calls a "strong delusion." Embracing delusion as truth is a most dangerous exercise; it is the prelude to judgment and inevitable damnation (2 Thessalonians 2:11).

Society is moving into a narrow valley of fate. Its position is becoming increasingly perilous as it follows the fantasies of an existential world view. To those who subscribe to such thinking, the individual moment has no causes and no consequences. There is no heaven to gain or hell to shun. The call is to "Do it now! Enjoy it now! There is no tomorrow, so go for all you can get today!" Losing its concept of eternity, our generation has traded the doctrine of moral responsibility for that of instant gratification. This doctrine offers enjoyment at the beginning but entombment in the end. The law of diminishing returns, however, has now begun to set in. Politicians and philosophers labor to hide the truth of our deteriorating condition, but such a huge issue cannot be concealed. The crucial issues of our time—Communism, the resurgence of Islam, the turbulence in the Middle East, Liberation Theology, the threat of global economic collapse, the AIDS epidemic, the staggering pileup of nuclear weapons—are progressing to the point that any one could end our present form of civilization.

Yet society—irrational and blind by choice—continues to minimize its peril and promise utopia. Even the church has been drawn into these delusions. We might hope that believers would make no such mistake. But many who profess faith in Christ have also become "presentists." This moment is everything and eternity, if it exists, is irrelevant. Various new theologies have stolen away the emphasis on personal salvation and eternal life. They have substituted social change and economic reward as the true benefits of Christianity. The reality of eternity has given way to the importance of time. The treasures of earth and the approval of men have relegated the golden streets in the New Jerusalem to the level of a childhood bedtime story.

Nevertheless, after all the speeches about "human possibilities" and "permanent gains," the reality of humanity's temporal condition remains. The days pass, the months expire, the years flourish and fail. How soon the world forgets, as Tennyson said, that "our little systems have their day,/They have their day and cease to be."

The world emphasizes the present because it misunderstands the nature of time. We must remember that the past no longer exists; we have no influence over it. And the present is but a fleeting instant, not a thing of permanence. We can photograph this moment, but we cannot keep it. The only dimension of time that continues to exist is the future, and we can influence the future. In fact, our actions have significance only as they relate to the future. To concern ourselves with the future and our place in it is called planning.

Peter invites us to plan the future by building "these things" into our lives. Notice again the promise that "if these things be in you, and abound" (2 Peter 1:8), you will avoid spiritual failure. There awaits for you a glorious entrance into the everlasting kingdom of our Lord.

"In you" are the important words. We must ask, "Are these things truly in me?" Even as we have considered these eight imperatives, we know the answer to this question. If deep within my soul I find doubt, cynicism, and indulgence rather than faith and virtue, "these things" are not within.

We must further make sure that these things "abound" in our lives. Faith, even a small amount of faith, is the basis of our salvation. But abounding faith spills out from our lives and into the thirsting lives of others. Virtue purifies the person who makes it his practice. When virtue abounds, however, it becomes salt and light in society.

These imperatives must become more than commitments. They must be our life's enthusiasm. They must abound!

When they abound, they profoundly influence both time and eternity for the one who has pursued these imperatives. It is then they guarantee a most brilliant future. The believer, so endowed, will shine as the stars forever and ever. This eternal luminescence that the committed believer takes to himself will become apparent to all at a most momentous occasion that will take place in the beginning of our experience in heaven. That occasion is called the judgment seat of Christ. Concerning this, the Scripture says, "For we must appear before the judgment seat of Christ; that every one may receive the things done in his body, according to that he hath done" (2 Corinthians 5:10).

Many believers, when they anticipate seeing Christ, have the image of a gentle Jesus, meek and mild. They imagine the one they have seen pictured in the pages of a childhood Bible. But to anticipate Christ's appearance on that basis is inadequate.

God has provided us with a vivid description of Christ's appearance in heaven. The apostle John, in the concluding book of Scripture, titled "The Revelation of Jesus Christ," gives us that description:

> And I turned to see the voice that spake with me. And being turned, I saw seven golden candlesticks; and in the midst of the seven candlesticks, one like unto the Son of man, clothed with a garment down to the foot, and girt about the paps with a golden girdle. His head and his hairs were white like wool, as white as snow; and his eyes were as a flame of fire; And his feet like unto fine brass, as if they burned in a furnace; and his voice as the sound of many waters. And he had in his

right hand seven stars: and out of his mouth went a sharp twoedged sword: and his countenance was as the sun shineth in his strength. (Revelation 1:12-16)

The prospect of standing before such magnificence is not to be contemplated lightly. We do well to note John's reaction, especially in light of the fact that he had walked for three years in fellowship with Christ on earth. On a human level, he knew Christ well. Nevertheless, he said, "And when I saw him, I fell at his feet as dead. And he laid his right hand upon me, saying unto me, Fear not; I am the first and the last: I am he that liveth, and was dead; and, behold, I am alive for evermore, Amen; and have the keys of hell and death" (vv. 17-18).

As it was with the apostle John, so it must be with you and me. Before that awesome throne and that King, you *must* appear! I *must* appear! We shall not fail that appointment. Considering that occasion, we do well to ask, What will it be like? Am I prepared?

It will, of course, be like nothing we have seen. When we appear before that throne we will answer for all we have said, thought, planned, or done. The thoughts, actions, and activities of each believer will be shown for what they *truly* are. They will be visible as gold, silver, and precious stones, or they will be revealed as wood, hay, and stubble. The works of every child of God will be tried by fire and the fire will reveal what sort they are. The works of some will survive; the works of some will be consumed.

In the light of this final evaluation, we do well to ask, What works of mine will be gold? What will be silver? What diamonds or rubies will I have to present to Him?

The works of enduring value will be the ones associated with "these things"—those characterized by faith, virtue, knowledge, self-control, patience, godliness, brotherly kindness, and love.

Being convinced of the importance of the judgment seat of Christ, we may rejoice in the instructions we are given. We are told of the credentials we must have in order to anticipate our Lord's approval. These credentials are not secret, mysterious, or incomprehensible. They are stated for all. They are the imperatives of spiritual success. And we do not pursue them alone but with the help of the indwelling Spirit of the living God.

As Peter concludes his treatment of the imperatives, he warns us of the onrushing future by saying, "We have also a more sure word of prophecy; whereunto ye do well that ye take heed, as unto a light that shineth in a dark place, until the day dawn, and the day star arise in your hearts" (2 Peter 1:19). As the dawn of eternity approaches, we must build these qualities within our lives.

Peter goes on to warn us of the spiritual subversion to come. He waves the red flag by saying, "There shall be false teachers among you, who [secretly] shall bring in damnable heresies, even denying the Lord that bought them, and bring upon themselves swift destruction" (2 Peter 2:1). Many will follow fatal paths. This warning, occupying a whole chapter in Peter's letter, reminds us of the necessity of living for and preaching the truth. The time is coming when people will not endure sound doctrine. The best way to avoid spiritual subversion is by having the imperatives built into our lives.

He turns next to the end of the world and the events to come, which he calls "the day of the Lord." "The heavens shall pass away with a great noise, and the elements shall melt with fervent heat, the earth also and the works that are therein shall be burned up" (2 Peter 3:10). The material things people have devoted their lives to —the cars, the clothes, the houses, the diamonds, the rep-

utations, the successes—will be gone forever. Only spiritual qualities will continue to have value. In fact, Peter
says, "Seeing then that all these things shall be dissolved,
what manner of persons ought ye to be in all holy conversation and godliness, looking for and hasting unto the
coming of the day of God" (vv. 3:11-12).

How soon will this day come upon us? We do not
know, but we do know that sinful man has now taken
into his trembling hands the equipment of devastation
that could bring it to pass.

What, then, really matters in life? It is "holy conversation and godliness." Although this may seem like
prudishness or an abstraction, it is exactly the opposite.
It is the fabric of eternity, fabric that will endure after the
world is gone.

We are to refuse the temptation to live for the things
that will soon pass away. The gold of this world will one
day melt and run like mud through the streets of the
flaming cities of earth. The passion for pursuing wealth
will be shown to be without eternal value. The things of
eternal value are spiritual. They are immaterial and the
most solid, the most real things of all.

Spiritual success is the one thing in life without
which nothing else is of genuine or lasting value. "These
things" therefore—faith, virtue, knowledge, self-control,
patience, godliness, brotherly kindness, love—must never be viewed as options within the Christian life. They
are vital and achievable. They are the keys to a life lived
for eternity.